I CHOOSE ME

The Intentional Guide To Never Losing Yourself Again

JINEEN R. HUFF

I Choose Me
The Intentional Guide To Never Losing Yourself Again

Copyright © 2023 by Intentional Queen Journey, LLC.

Published by Intentional Queen Journey Media
Printed in the United States of America

www.intentionalqueenjourney.com
info@intentionalqueenjourney.com

Cover Photo Image: Tiffany Simmons

1st edition, December 2023
ISBN: 979-8-9896493-0-3 (eBook)
ISBN: 979-8-9896493-1-0 (Paperback Print)

DEDICATION

This book is dedicated to the younger version of myself and any Intentional Queen that identifies with my story. You are inspiring for impact, and your journey is about helping women no longer suffer in silence. You are the light, so keep shining through adversity! Enjoy the next chapter in your life!

This book is also dedicated to my son. Being your mom is one of the best gifts God has given me. You are loved, smart, and a child of God. Forever, you will be my baby!

CONTENTS

Part 4: Blooming into Your Soft Woman Season (Butterfly Transformation)

INTRODUCTION

Hi there! Have you at times felt like you were not able to show up as your true, authentic self? Maybe it was due to a fear of not belonging or of making others feel uncomfortable? Or maybe you felt like your voice didn't matter? Or maybe because you were not listened to in the past as a younger person, you don't feel confident that others will listen to you now, even though you have so much to share?

It's not a good feeling at all and can feel like you have to shrink and be a chameleon in settings where you really just want to be yourself. I want to help you overcome this. And believe me, you can!

But first, I'd like to share with you a bit about how I came to help others to feel the joy of being totally themselves.

My family and I always knew I was different since I was a little girl. I distinctly have memories of me complaining to my parents when I was a child about the challenges, I was constantly facing due to my high aspirations and dreams.

You see, I've always been a driven and self-disciplined person. I wouldn't let anyone, or anything stop me from my goals! And even if it meant that I had to do it alone. I believe that having this mindset has served me well in certain areas of my life, and I'm grateful for that, but I realized as I grew into womanhood, that some of these beliefs no longer served me. It was time for a change.

So, I went on a mission to show up for myself with more confidence, restore wholeness within, and let my light shine on in the world. A pretty important mission, wouldn't you say? We do only have this one precious life, and I was determined to make the very best of it. I'm so lucky to have wonderful parents that have been my biggest cheerleaders. I know now everyone has that. They even told me that one day I would write a book to help people based on my life experiences. And here I am! But years ago, I didn't believe them. I just couldn't see it. And today, I'm sitting here sharing my life experiences, because I want more women to feel empowered enough to let their own lights shine and embrace their true identities, and without shame!

Remember that life is a journey. It will require you to evolve and change just like the seasons. This is one of the reasons why I am so fond of the stunning transformation of butterflies.

Intentional Queen Journey was birthed by allowing my tests to become testimonies to help others who have felt silenced and at a crossroads in their lives. Speaking my voice with authority also allowed me to heal, restore, and empower others to do the same with God's grace. Never forget that there is so much power in your voice and story. So, make sure you stand in your truth!

Simply by having faith as small as a mustard seed, you can transform and restore your life. You absolutely can. I've done it, and I've seen it in others, and what a joy it is to witness! The goal is simple: to become whole and heal the broken pieces in order to level up to become a better version of yourself in your next season. We must remember here that the seasons change, with or without our acceptance. So, we must evolve with the seasons, always looking forward.

And when you do so, you will love yourself through a different lens. This will allow you to break free from your cocoon and then fly freely with a more peaceful, fulfilling life.

During my journey, I became intentional about all things in my life, personally and professionally. I no longer apologize for being who God made me to be, nor did I dim my light to make others feel comfortable. As a result, I have become more comfortable in my own skin and show up for myself because I know my self-worth. But part of embracing your own growth during the journey is knowing that you must give yourself grace and let go of perfectionism. A tough one, I know!

If you're trying to figure out where to start, know it starts from within you and your mindset. It starts with having intentional thoughts. I do know and understand that any kind of vulnerability, and acknowledging one's flaws or admitting that we need help is challenging. Many of us fear failure and we fear showing up as our true selves. And if you've been hiding your true self for a long time, it's even harder. I've been there. But once I began to let down that mask, I gained greater fulfillment in my life and began to embrace my authentic self.

> *I felt free like a butterfly bursting out of a cocoon, ready to take flight!*

This came from me pushing past the fear of the unknown and continuously affirming myself along the way. My podcast is a prime example of faithing it through fear because it was trying something new that I didn't have any previous experience with. Plus, it was totally unrelated to my nursing career! But we surprise ourselves with what we can do once we give it a chance.

Change may feel scary because it's stepping out of our comfort zones, but eventually, you build up confidence by continuing to be courageous! As adults, we can get caught in the trap of complacency and we like things to remain the same because it gives us a sense of control and comfort. However, most fulfillment and growth are achieved outside of our comfort zones.

> *"It takes 21 days to learn a new habit." - Dr. Maxwell Maltz*

Give yourself grace during your time of adjustment. Continue to be consistent and show up for yourself daily. For example, speaking positive affirmations, being present now, and having self-discipline. And go easy on yourself too. Don't give up if you've had a few setbacks - that's normal!

When you start positively talking back to your inner critic and become more courageous and surer of yourself, you will improve your self-belief and your confidence levels will rise.

Keep in mind that vulnerability and healing can be messy. You will have high and low moments. But you must trust the process. Love yourself first and remember that you are enough today.

This book is for you, and for all the women who are courageous enough to tap into their own vulnerability. To have a try at shifting her limited beliefs and letting go of what no longer serves her.

Love who you are without being apologetic about it!

This book will be your self-love guide on how to show up more confidently and whole in every area of your life with intentionality, grace, authenticity, and humility, as you break free from your cocoon and begin pivoting into the more peaceful life you desire.

Remember that being intentional about what we do is a journey, not a destination. I hope when you read this book, you'll know this to be true and adopt these positive intentions in your own life. Shine your light bright, so everyone else can see it too!

Also available is the *Ready To Thrive 3-Day Challenge,* where you learn how to feel less overwhelmed, discover inner peace, and embrace self-love! Join this free email challenge today at https://intentionalqueenjourney.com/readytothrive/.

PART ONE

NAVIGATE LIFE'S CROSSROADS IN THE PURSUIT OF SUCCESS

CHAPTER 1
Get to the Roots

We're back walking down memory lane (cue music). Picture this; a four-year-old little girl taking care of her dolls like they were real people and telling everyone she was going to be a nurse when she grows up.

Yes, that was me! And yes, I knew what educational journey I needed to become a nurse at a very young age!

My motivation, determination, perseverance, tenacity, strength, and discipline have been unapparelled since I was a teenager. I have always been someone who was goal-oriented and ready to just get things done with my own free will and grit.

I remember being valedictorian of my high school class and the only student who ever received this honor in the Practical Nursing Program at that high school during that time. The Practical Nursing Program was a very intense, a college prep program at my vocational high school. I did well. My instructors told my parents that once I understood the subject matter, I was going to be among the elite.

I had some pretty high demands on me during that time with academics and clinical duties. Not to mention that I had a part-time job after school - why? Because I like making money!

> *But all of this put together placed a crazy amount of pressure stress and anxiety on me in order for me to function at my highest level in every area of my life. I definitely had perfectionistic tendencies, to say the least.*

I wanted my grades to be stellar, not to mention my organizational skills. I was the one you came looking to for good notes and key information that was color-coded! Yep, I was that girl.

I mean, I have always been an organized and structured person. I think it is also how I was raised by my parents.

But I am very, very organized. I believe it can be a gift and a curse! I love google calendars, spreadsheets, the BIC (4-color clickable pen), planners, post-notes and highlighters. Aren't they the best? I get excited during back-to-school sales to reload my office supplies. I love watching home organizing shows on tv and cleaning hacks on TikTok.

My friends say I should have been a lawyer and home organizer because of my attention to detail and organization. I do feel that everything needs a place, because if there's things all over the place, I find it stressful. Clutter truly does affect my peace!

I do talk more about my past perfectionistic ways throughout the book, and how I was able to promote ease/boost productivity by letting it not run me! because yes, I do recognize there is a difference between being super organized, and letting it take over your life and become a stress in itself.

I had an organized filing system with labels for each lesson plan. My planner and phone calendar were color-coded to reflect what was urgent, things to do, appointments, work, and tasks. This is still something I do to this day to keep me organized. One of my closets is for dressy clothing and the other is for casual clothing. The list can go on forever, but these are just to name a few.

I remember being voted "Most Likely to Succeed" in our yearbook. The funniest thing of all is that I wasn't your typical nerd! I hung out with the cool crowds and dressed stylishly. You could say I learned how to be a chameleon at a young age. I grew up in the mid-80's, so I watched the TV show "Family Matters" with Steve Urkel and Stefan Urkel. Stefan was the cool version of Steve Urkel. In school, I was the female version of Stefan Urkel, charismatic and smart at the same time. I didn't wear glasses or have a pocket protector. I loved to get my nails done and have stylish hairdos (but just peek inside my bag - total nerd!). My favorite stores doing that time for fashion were *Rainbow* and *5-7-9*! If you grew up in my era, then you already know those were the stores to shop for the latest trends.

I've always been eager to learn and do whatever I set my mind to, to the best of my ability.

Failure was never an option for me, and neither was quitting, even if it was difficult.

On the flip side, this made some people envious of my accolades, which made me want to shrink in order to make others feel comfortable being around me. I was raised to not talk about myself because people can interpret it as bragging or boasting, even if I was celebrating my own win. Imagine having awards and trophies that were hidden away in a box that only you knew existed? Or better yet, having a hidden treasure where you knew the value, but you didn't want others to try to take advantage of your worth.

Truthfully, I didn't like giving unnecessary attention to myself. I loved those dramas and movies like *Scarface* and *American Gangster*; keeping a low profile can keep the haters and the "shade" away. "Shade" is that feeling, vibe, or snicker you get when someone is annoyed at your achievements, we've all seen it. The way some people have a way of being dismissive or giving back-handed compliments to try to diminish your success because they are uncomfortable with your growth. Instead, it simply shines a light on their flaws and brings forth their insecurities.

But this way of thinking would start to affect how I would show up in my personal and professional relationships. When you are a child, you yearn for acceptance, not adversity or being different. Little offences can lead to big ones if not dealt with over time.

During my high school graduation speech, I spoke about my challenging journey of wanting to everything so perfectly. I also wanted to highlight the importance of making sure we slow down and smell the roses before moving on to the next goal in life. However, I didn't fully apply these strategies until later in my adulthood. Let's just say God has a way of taking over when you don't heed his instructions to slow down!

The Mission to Find Me Again

I implore everyone to slow down and smell the roses of this accomplishment as we embark on new journeys into adulthood!

Over 20 years later, I still reflect on these words spoken during my valedictorian speech about slowing down and enjoying the little things in life. As I said, in high school, I had pushed myself very hard to be perfect and never really enjoyed each accomplishment. It was basically a goal checked off my list and then it was straight on to my next one. Reflecting on my mistakes in this respect reminds me that time is valuable and to enjoy the moment. It just goes so fast!

I needed to finally let go of making sure everything is perfect and let some things be simply 'good enough.' Because they were and are good enough! I am good enough – which is more what this is about.

We can sometimes get so bound to the image people have of us or even their opinions, that we cling to that, and try to mold ourselves into this unrealistic version that is not really who we are at all.

But because of this pattern, I'd come to live by, made becoming a more intentional person a whole lot more challenging and caused an inner battle of conflict. It meant I desired to have an intentional shift in my perspective and believe in myself on a deeper level for the new chapter in my life but doing that was a whole other thing to be able to do. To heal and grow from the inside out! To take up space and show up for myself. My real self.

> ## I wanted to BREAK FREE of the mask and be Jineen!

Now, the feeling of not being stuck forever anymore was a great feeling that I had yearned for so, so long. But the next challenge was to actually do it.

I wanted and needed a strategy on how to release and purge things that no longer served me. I was more than ready for it. But I knew it was going to take some inner work and finding peace within myself.

I realized that wanting something is not enough, I knew I was still struggling to be present in different areas of my life and not trusting God to help me in my adulthood. Over the years, I'd been working multiple high-stress jobs and in settings that lacked diversity on a regular basis as an Advanced Practice Registered nurse. This can be taxing to your mental state because there were many times when I had to shrink to make others feel comfortable or not want to cause too much attention for fear of not belonging. Not to mention sometimes the fear of possible retaliation.

And for those reasons, instead of saying *"NO"*, I would say *"Sure, yes, and okay!"* It was just easier to go with the flow and keep the peace.

So, there I was giving all my energy to people and things. Slowly pouring out my time and energy without refilling myself while I was at it. Yes, I was so misguided, but we live, and we learn. This is actually a common trait for healthcare and other high-achieving professionals to lack or have minimal self-care routines. Interesting, when those are the ones who need it most. There seems to be a common thread of not recognizing their capacity and struggling with boundaries.

When you are a high-achieving professional, you tend to work extra hard on your job to get promoted, you go over and beyond for others, and become agreeable in order to appear as the "good" employee. Then you exert all your energy and mental peace on your job and have minimal energy for your personal life when you go home. You're mentally and physically exhausted. And as a result, your personal relationships and overall well-being begin to deteriorate because of the constant hamster wheel of never taking a break or doing things that fill your soul. You miss important events and quality time with the people you love the most because of tiredness and overwhelm. Not to mention the shame and guilt you feel when you feel like you are not doing a good job at balancing your life and taking care of yourself. Whereas you may feel you're doing a great job in some areas, you're lacking awfully in others. And you know it.

If you're a people pleaser, like I was, be aware that people-pleasing may avoid some initial discomfort but can be detrimental to your psyche long term because you are basically not honoring and loving yourself.

Sit with that for a moment!

I knew I was rushing through my life and not smelling the roses! Stretching myself too thin! Struggling to balance work, home life, and motherhood.

Like so many of us trying to figure out how to live life in this crazy-busy demanding modern life, somewhere along the lines, I lost myself.

Who was Jineen, without her titles?

And because I wasn't sure who she was, it led to burnout.

But this was a gift. It helped me to (or shall I say, forced me to) become more self-aware of my habits and tendencies toward perfectionism and stretching myself too thinly posed a real threat to my overall health and well-being.

I mean, I was definitely considered high-functioning in every area of my life, successful, like I had it all together and, on the outside, looked like I was nailing all areas of my life. But at what cost in the long run?! And that is what needs to be calculated carefully.

It's funny because even to this day, people call me "Checklist!" I think that comes from having over twenty years of a nursing career and being a process-oriented thinker. I was always taught that protocols and checklists decreased the risks of errors and promoted patient safety!

So naturally, I have been accustomed to adopting this in my daily habits of discipline and intentional living. Again, I believe it can be a gift and a curse because it can lead to perfectionism. I am hypervigilant and love things to be organized into categories. My brain computes data that way and it helps me function in chaos with a sense of order. But the fact is, life isn't always ordered. I like clean, organized spaces, even in my work environment. People are drawn to me for my organizational and planning skills. And if you meet my parents, you will understand where my siblings and I get it from! Oh, how similar we can be to our parents, as much as we try to deny it!

I worked throughout the pandemic. It was natural. My attitude toward being a grinder goes as far back as I can remember. Working while being in school was a given, and while I got my college degrees, I've always had at least two to three jobs at one time.

You may ask why. Why did I push myself to such limits?!

Well, I always had a vision about where I wanted to go, and I was willing to sacrifice temporarily to create the life I envisioned…the house, car, family, legacy, debt-free, etc.!

All the things you hear as a little girl that womanhood should be. I am not sure if these images in society were actually correct or true depictions. In fact, of course, I know that they are not. Life is not a fairytale. But kids are so impressionable at an early age, and we are taught that we, as women can have it all. What a lie! What a way to set them up for failure when they can't keep every ball in the air.

I don't regret my vision at that tender age, but I do reflect on my motives and some misconceptions that don't serve me anymore. It's wonderful to have dreams, we all need them, but the truth hits that much harder if we don't know a bit of the reality facing us.

But the fast pace and all that grit were wearing me down mentally and physically. I was having challenges in some of my personal and professional relationships due to my burnout from stretching myself thin while trying to do it all. I wasn't functioning at my best self, so people around me were beginning to suffer too.

Ultimately, I was not living a fulfilled life on my terms and finally decided that I wanted a more peaceful life. Enough was enough.

So how do you know if you're not operating as your best self?

Well, it may show up as feeling overwhelmed, stressed, or struggling to balance various responsibilities. You might feel like you're constantly putting others' needs before your own, leading to burnout and exhaustion. You may feel resentful, anxious, or angry.

This is important to change because neglecting your own well-being can impact your ability to support others effectively, and it can hinder personal growth and happiness. By embracing self-care and knowing your capacity to hold, you can improve your overall well-being and be more present and empowered in your life. And the result is a happier you, and happier people around you.

Being a caregiver all day, every day can become taxing, not to mention the high panic of the pandemic in the healthcare industry during that time. It was tough! The juggle got even bigger.

I do believe though, that God has a way of slowing you down if you don't give yourself permission to do so. I came to the realization that my body was shutting down and sending me indicators that my capacity was very low. I was basically running on empty. And of course, I was. I was never refilling my own cup.

It started when I looked in the mirror and noticed my eyes and neck size beginning to enlarge from my thyroid gland. That was a shock! Thyroid disease runs in my family and usually is triggered by high levels of stress that affect your metabolism. My weight was fluctuating, and my blood pressure was elevated too. All serious signs of burnout.

I cried in the bathroom that day because I heard my mom's voice in my head!

> *Stress can harm or kill you. Never let anyone or anything stress you out to the point that you suffer. You must let it, or them, go immediately!*

These are all the things she used to warn me about as a little girl and now, finally, I heard it loud and clear from one who knew it all too well herself. My mother has faced her own trials with thyroid disease related to stress and burnout, so I knew what this potentially meant for me!

So, I booked a doctor's appointment and physical to be evaluated for my symptoms. They ran multiple tests and did ultrasounds of my neck. I was even having trouble swallowing and experiencing high levels of fatigue, even with rest. This was not good! And this is when I knew things were getting real in these streets. I had to go on medication temporarily and have my lab values checked frequently.

I was told to slow down and rest. But resting has always been a point of contention for me! I like to be always on the go and on to the next thing. I realized though that that is what led me to being in this position.

It's the pitfall of being a high-functioning woman and embracing the "Superwoman" mentality! It's just not viable long-term.

> *The message had finally sunk in. It was time for self-care and prioritizing my own needs; these were a necessity that became an integral part of my lifestyle.*

I began evaluating everything and everyone in my life to get to the roots of my stress and pivot toward peace. I have learned that I am not replaceable, and I must take care of myself first. There may be no second chances. We only have one life, and what if I ruin mine by continuing this misguided path? Also, I knew I had to be more proactive about asking for what I need and to ask for it from the people who have the capacity to fulfill those needs. That is a form of self-love.

CHAPTER 2

Identify Your Catalysts (Causes)

Catalysts are pivotal moments in your life when you approach a crossroads or big hurdle you must overcome in the pursuit of success. You can identify that you're undergoing a pivot when you're faced with significant choices that have the potential to profoundly affect your overall welfare and the people in your vicinity.

At life's crossroads, you have a multitude of directions to choose from – left, right, back, forward, or even taking a moment to stand still. Embrace this critical juncture as an opportunity to delve deeper into yourself, discern your true desires, and confidently navigate the path that aligns with your purpose.

I believe that you know you're at a crossroads when something in your spirit says you're not in alignment with what's happening. You have doubts and concerns, and you want things to change.

My parents used to give certain words of wisdom to my siblings and I over the years, but there was one thing that was sticking out to me during that time.

> *You come to a point in your life when you get sick and tired of being sick and tired! And when you become sick and tired of being sick and tired, you normally do something about it!*

This is when you are perpetually going through a cycle that needs to change, such as insanity.

> *Yes, insanity is doing the same thing over and over again expecting a different result.*

You come to a point in your life where you realize something just has to change! This will help free you from continuously being in a state of insanity.

Insanity can be mind-blowing because sometimes you don't even realize that you are in a vicious, toxic cycle.

But there comes a time when you must face the pivotal moments in life and identify the underlying driving force behind them.

Catalysts by definition are things that cause something to happen or a reaction to occur. It's the beginning or deep root of something that leads you to get to the crossroads or intersection in life.

Your catalysts can be very covert or overt, meaning that they could be things you don't see. Or you may know them in your heart to be true, but you don't physically see them manifesting. You may also know they are there but actively ignore them or are in denial because you don't want to face the truth. Also, very common!

Sure, you can ignore them, push them back down, but they will begin to show up in other ways if they are not addressed.

Therefore, in the following chapter, I will discuss the consequential effects, or byproducts, of these catalysts.

You Must Address Them!

During conversations with accomplished women, I discovered that many of them had also encountered pain, trauma, or unresolved generational wounds that they had not addressed or resolved.

For example, they shared evidence of being in dysfunctional relationships or having inner child wounds that needed to be unpacked, that were possibly festering, too. They shared feelings regarding past generations raising them to be silent, to be seen and not heard and the effects of that. Or being told to tolerate things that maybe they should not have or should have confronted.

These women also expressed concerns about struggling to adjust to new life events such as marriage, having children, death, or divorce. I can identify with all four of these new life events!

Such experiences in particular can contribute to feeling overwhelmed and excessively burdened. As an introvert, I personally leaned towards maintaining a low profile, not allowing others to witness the challenges occurring in my personal life.

I am no therapist, but my life coaching career and over twenty years of nursing experience have helped me recognize the correlation with some of these common struggles.

Personally, I think, if you can, it is healthy to have a therapist and a life coach. They serve two different roles in your life and give you a much-needed boost in the right direction and keep you on track.

Mental health is so very important!

I think I've made that pretty clear by now, but it deserves another mention!

The power lies truly lies in you, to attain peace of mind and cultivate a mindful state of being.

Three years ago, my word of the year was 'pivot', and my ultimate goal was pivoting towards peace! Do you like it? Feel free to steal it! I went on a mission to make sure that if something was going to disturb my inner peace, it was going to be purged! But first, I made sure to identify what I had capacity for in my daily life. This may not seem such a big deal, but it really was for someone like me who thought I could take on way too much. But I got better at it, and realized that if something was disturbing my well-being, it was an indicator that a boundary was needed in that particular area, or that something had to change, and fast.

This is why I became a Mindset Coach and Self-Love Expert! I wanted to help others lift themselves up from being stuck in the same spot I was.

So many people suffer in silence and live with A.N.T.S. (automatic negative thoughts) in their minds, which can lead to such suffering, to such a detriment to their lives, and in the worst-case scenario, suicide.

A therapist can give you the gift of helping you unpack and heal old wounds from past struggles or trauma that are holding you back. To be honest, you pay them to listen to you complain and express what is bothering you without bias. It's awesome! And unlike dear friends who tend to let us keep a few things buried, a therapist has the experience to help gently guide you to take a good look at what's going on in your day-to-day life, and below the surface.

Your family and friends will get tired of you bringing up the same stuff over time. And while they may be a great listener and supporter, they don't have the skills to help you move forward.

If this is you, please seek your own therapist because your family will thank you for it too! No more venting a little too much! Sure, everyone who loves you wants to help but they too can feel a bit helpless when they aren't able to help you move past the venting stage to the taking-action stage.

Because when you carry unhealed emotional wounds, it can lead to bleeding on others, causing your pain to impact those around you if not properly addressed.

> **On the other hand, a life coach takes the remnants or pieces left after you heal and helps you move forward in life. They have the skills and experience to help you move forward and take action but also are not too personally involved.**

Basically, they help you to excavate what it is you want in your life and help you rebuild the life you want on your terms, so you can break out of the cocoon to become a butterfly!

They are your cheat code because they have perhaps been where you are, or at least have walked and lot of people through the process before you, and they know what works and doesn't work. They have the blueprint! Plus, they provide you with accountability along the way.

So, I received this revelation when I went through my own therapy and life coaching journey. It definitely served me well. I was so grateful! It was at that moment, I which realized that it was God's calling for me to serve as a motivational speaker, utilizing my influential voice to support and uplift others, just as I had been helped myself.

You see, The Intentional Queen Podcast: 'Journey to Restoration with Jineen' emerged three years ago as my personal endeavor to bring healing to others while simultaneously finding healing for myself.

My therapist actually had a candid conversation with me prior to my podcast launch. She expressed that by ceasing to shrink and embracing vulnerability, my personal stories would serve as testimonies that could profoundly impact and assist others. Her suggestion resonated deeply with me, prompting me to purchase a copy of Brene Brown's book, "The Power of Vulnerability," after our session. After reading this book, I felt compelled to keep going with my podcast episodes in a space of gratitude and vulnerability with my audience.

Even to this day, that single conversation has remained etched in my memory.

I never looked back or questioned my purpose for the podcast after the first few months of launching! And I gradually developed a greater sense of ease and dared myself to embrace vulnerability, while committing to showing up consistently and authentically for anyone who needed me.

It became evident to me that podcasting served as the gateway to my journey of becoming a life and mindset coach.

Looking ahead a few years from the launch of my podcast, I have since become a Certified Life Coach, empowering ambitious women worldwide to transform their mindsets and embark on their personal journeys of restoration. I couldn't be happier! This transformation was made possible by simply prioritizing my own growth, embracing authenticity, and consistently showing up for myself and others.

This transformation allows the healed version of me to intentionally impact everyone around me, especially my child in a positive manner.

> *My mantra is to inspire for impact and be there for the one person who needs me!*

These invaluable lessons I've acquired now inspire me to urge others (you!) to embark on your own journey of embracing vulnerability through inner introspection and personal growth.

Vulnerability can make you go into a space of digging deep. It can be unpleasant, it can be intense, but understand it is a necessary process you must go through to help free yourself and let others know they are not alone along the way.

The introspection of vulnerability allowed me to have more courage and share about real life topics that women encounter, some of which are taboo in my culture. I believe the candid conversations I have with my clients have reinforced the need to discuss and empower each other on how to overcome common struggles. To not keep these struggles hidden, to not have to try to deal with everything alone. Being raised in an extremely private setting presented one of the most challenging obstacles I faced in embracing my own vulnerability.

But if I can do it, I know you can too!

Purpose in Pain

Breaking generational curses or cycles can be hard because you become the change agent! It's when you declare that the cycle stops with you and any generations afterward. And that's exciting, isn't it?

This could also resemble breaking away from things and patterns that you've known all your life, and that have been practiced for generations. And becoming comfortable with this discomfort and pruning!

Rose bushes need to be pruned back, so they can flourish in their next season. Although the act of trimming lifeless foliage with pruning shears may initially inflict pain, it serves a greater purpose in the end.

Even if that means you lose people that were like your "decade" people!

"Decade" people are individuals who have been part of your life for years, and you initially expected them to accompany you into your next chapter. However, you come to realize that sometimes, in some cases, you need to leave them behind. This transition can sometimes evoke survivor's remorse, a sense of guilt or conflict that arises when you achieve success while others in your life are struggling or experiencing lack.

Note that at some point in your life, your circle will become smaller. Not always but is often the case when one person levels up. And that's okay.

Quality is better than quantity!

Think about a dime, for instance. Despite being the smallest coin, it's worth exceeds that of a penny or a nickel.

Make sure you know your worth!

During a networking session with other ambitious women, I heard them loud and clear as they also shared their own encounters with generational or traumatic experiences, including single motherhood, divorce, toxic relationships, grief, infertility, poverty, and various other challenges. Even just the day-to-day juggling of life and motherhood can be an immense challenge if we are not supported or if we feel our parenting choices don't match our upbringing or the choices of our friends. But at some point, we need to trust our intuition and go our own way.

The moments that left the strongest imprint of trauma on me were those connected to the process of grieving.

Remember: There will be purpose in your pain!

I will now recount some of the most challenging experiences I have faced and successfully overcome, as they have played a significant role in shaping me into the woman I am today. By sharing my testimonies, I aim to inspire and encourage you to persevere in your own journey.

Let's be clear, this is not the Jineen most people would describe over five years ago and remember that growth occurs while in motion!

It was in the midst of my transition into a new job that I experienced the sudden and unexpected loss of my cousin due to a health complication. Our bond was so close that we considered each other as sisters, having been raised together like siblings. From childhood, I acted as her voice and protector, and she was my trusted companion and confidante. Remarkably, we were the same age. Given her multiple health challenges, I occasionally shared candid discussions about her on my podcast.

And when I lost her, it was such a shock and devastation. She died alone on the couch. It still rocks me to my core. When I was going through the mud as I call it and experiencing grief, I missed her so much, but I was also smacked with the reality check too, that you can be young and still die!

Through this experience, I came to realize that nothing in life is guaranteed.

You don't get time back because it's that valuable!

And the unfortunate reality is that you might depart from this world, leaving your young children behind when they still greatly rely on you for their well-being and survival. In fact, they will always need you.

> *Faced with this reality, one that we naturally tend to avoid facing, we may contemplate; what have I invested in for my child and building a legacy?*

This is a good question that I recommend you should marinate on from time to time.

Since that heartbreaking experience, I began utilizing my time more wisely and going on a mission to build my own legacy for my family.

I still miss my cousin daily! I firmly hold the belief that she is with me in spirit, and her life holds profound meaning and purpose. Her sudden passing served as a catalyst in my life, signaling the need for a change and indicating that I was approaching a pivotal moment at the crossroads of my own journey. Yes, grief is an awfully sad but sneaky thing.

At times like this, we can keep in mind that within pain lies purpose. In fact, we must keep this in mind. Yet it is important to recognize and progress through the different stages of grief.

The last stage of grief is acceptance.

In addition to losing my cousin, I also experienced the loss of a child during pregnancy. This story holds great power as it taught me the importance of disregarding others' opinions and instead listening and trusting in what God says about me.

I don't look like what I have been through!

Let me explain. I remember when I was pregnant with my son who's now a first grader. Unknowingly, I was having twins and lost the twin baby early in my pregnancy.

I miscarried the baby while at work doing anaesthesia in the middle of a code-blue situation. From what I recall, I was on a 24-hour shift running to an emergency in the middle of the night. While placing a breathing tube into a critically-ill patient, blood was running down my legs and coming through my blue scrubs. The other technicians in the room recognized that there was something wrong but not me; I was focused on my task.

I suffered in silence by helping the patient and going to my call room shortly afterward. I began cleaning myself up and reading up on my symptoms. I was the only anesthesia provider in the hospital that night. I was praying and waiting for my now ex-husband to wake up since it happened in the middle of the night.

I remember being so happy that I was pregnant! I wasn't telling a lot of people because I was scared that I wouldn't maintain a pregnancy through the first trimester.

After getting off work, I went to the doctor that morning and the doctor told me that I had lost the baby from such a large amount of blood loss. I was in disbelief because, in my spirit, God told me I needed to ask for more testing. Despite my doctor's opinion, I protested that I wanted more procedures and a further evaluation. I went on to get this extra testing done, and Lord behold I was still pregnant with one child and the other child was evacuated. So, can you see? It doesn't matter what people say or think!

> *When God puts something in your spirit, heart, and mind, it is for you to believe your own truth!*

I went for multiple procedures after that to maintain that pregnancy and make sure everything was going well with my son. However, my stressful professional and personal life demands were beginning to affect my pregnancy at the time. I had to take an early leave of absence from work and be on bed rest because of the enduring stress until the time of delivery.

Interestingly, when I went for the ultrasound to see my child in a later trimester, I had prayed before going in for God to send me a sign that my child was okay because, at that time, I didn't even know the sex of the baby. God and I had made a pact! I said if my child is okay, please have him or her wave at me during the ultrasound! My mom came to that ultrasound appointment with me. She was so excited because she had walked this walk with me as well. As soon as they put the ultrasound probe on my stomach, can you guess what happened? My son pulled his thumb out of his mouth and waved at me. I cried tears of joy because I didn't listen to them tell me months before that I was no longer pregnant with either child. But look at how God turns it around!

> *"Trust him and don't lean on your own understanding!"*
> *- Proverbs 3:5-6*

Those doctors never apologized to me, but I've learned to follow my instinct! That in itself was a blessing, and I began to walk by faith and not by sight. This is really when my walk with God became intentional and intimate! You have to find him for yourself and develop a relationship.

So, I gave birth to my son healthily, but it did cause me some post-partum depression. I sometimes think about the loss of the other child. But I also know everything happens for a reason and there was a reason that the other child was not viable. Embarking on a healing journey of gratitude and acceptance allowed me to flourish in my own circumstances and extend that same support to others.

Hurt People, Hurt People

Dysfunctional relationships can occur when you are choosing people because of broken places in your own life. At the time, you may not know why you chose them or better yet why they chose you! You may be walking around bleeding on people from your trauma or wounds. It happens, a lot. Sometimes others may be nurturing an unhealed version of you, but it is not until you evolve that you discover that it may be a relationship that no longer serves you. By delving deeper and accepting personal accountability, you will come to recognize the catalyst that influenced your decision to enter or prolong a relationship in the first place. This insight will tell you what you need to do.

The goal is to have healthy relationships with people in your life, but dysfunctional relationships can be between friends, family, and lovers.

I mean, of course, it is okay to have healthy disagreements, but it should not be a continuous, toxic situation.

> *Discovering what's toxic about it will help you to decide where you are in your journey to wholeness and what you need to do for your future. We all know deep down when something is not good for us.*

The thing is, when you begin to do the healing on the inside to allow time for full growth, you will be able to heal people as well. You have stopped bleeding on people and providing intentional support from a healed mindset. There is power of your mind. Be vigilant and wise when speaking with others.

Prioritize reflection before speaking to ensure that you leave people in the same or improved state as when you encountered them.

I firmly believe that those who have experienced healing have the ability to heal others by embodying authenticity and showing up as their true selves. This demonstrates to others that they are not alone and that you empathize with their challenges. Moreover, you can provide them with inspiration and hope, empowering them to shift their perspectives and overcome their own obstacles. They can see that if you can do it, perhaps they can too.

Unveiling the Inner Child

I have explored the concept that individuals who have experienced hurt and pain themselves often end up causing harm to others. And there does appear to be a pattern. However, it is essential to acknowledge that this behavior is often rooted in unresolved childhood wounds or personal challenges and that it can be overcome.

"When the little girl heals, the woman becomes whole."
- Vania Swain

Certain experiences from our childhood, even seemingly insignificant at the time, can serve as small seeds that grow and influence our adult lives. Just like weeds that start small before growing larger, it becomes essential to prioritize sowing positive seeds to outnumber and overcome any negative influences/weeds.

Exploring the depths of our inner child encourages us to recognize the significance of embracing vulnerability during our transformative journey. However, societal perceptions often discourage self-expression, as vulnerability is sometimes seen as a sign of weakness or timidity.

Growing up, my mother, a woman of strength and ambition, instilled in me a parenting approach characterized by structure and rigidity. Don't get me wrong, both of my parents were loving and compassionate! However, structure and routine were dominant in their parenting styles.

I was raised by my stepfather, a gentle and calm man of faith. He is also a military veteran, so you can see how this parenting style came naturally to him! I want everyone to know that this man always treated me as a princess and is still one of my biggest cheerleaders till this day! I believe in giving people their flowers while they are alive! I love you, Mom, and Dad! I guess now you are nodding and confirming the connection between myself and my parents. It's funny because I often tell people to meet my parents in order to understand some of my innate behaviors of structure and organization! As I've grown into adulthood, I've come to comprehend the reasons behind their parenting approach. In our private family, the vulnerability was not a commonly practiced trait. Now, I've come to the realization that the previous generations, including my parents, had valid reasons for their reluctance toward vulnerability. Their primary concern was ensuring our safety and well-being. Helping us to become strong. Understanding this, I can empathize with their choices and the intentions behind them.

Through my own example of leading with vulnerability, I have inspired and empowered my family to embrace their own openness and authenticity. I have witnessed the transformative power of vulnerability in my own life, as it requires courage to show up authentically and be true to oneself. By taking that initial step, even when it feels uncertain, we can gradually build confidence and navigate through life's challenges. It's about starting with faith and persevering until we make it, knowing that the journey toward growth and self-discovery is worth every moment of uncertainty.

> *Baby steps lead to giant leaps, so just keep going!*

I believe vulnerability unfolds in stages, and it's important to exercise discernment while navigating this process.

I want to share a transparency moment. I took a deliberate approach with my podcast, launching it three months before sharing it with my family and friends. I wanted to protect the authenticity of my vision and ensure that external opinions wouldn't sway or hinder its development. In fact, I intentionally chose not to display my face on the podcast cover, allowing listeners to connect with me beyond superficial judgments. I wanted to be a woman of impact! More importantly, I wanted to be obedient to God. I even have had the pleasure of my family sharing my podcasting space with me for a couple of personal conversations within the first year. But I needed to go at my own pace.

Empowering women globally through my message and supporting them in addressing their personal struggles has been an immense blessing. Sharing my own vulnerability and journey has not only enriched my own growth but has also inspired others to unpack their own baggage and experience transformative healing.

Plus, showing ambitious women how they can overcome obstacles by maximizing their faith and trusting the process, has been amazing. The debut of my first podcast episode marked a significant milestone in my journey, despite being a challenging one. It demanded vulnerability as I shared my story on a public platform, revealing my rawness and growth (the bruised caterpillar stage) for all to hear. However, after consistently showing up for three years, you can witness my evolution from a bruised caterpillar stage to a butterfly transformation in my personal life. Trust the process!

> *The beauty of the metamorphosis is that you don't look like you went into the cocoon when you come out flying free!*

My logo is a butterfly for this reason, with an "8" in the middle to represent the word journey!

Now, be mindful that some people may wish to hold you to your old version of yourself because they're not ready to accept the new version of you. And that is quite alright! And it's human nature for people to be unsure of change.

However, it takes time for them to accept who you have become. Give them time.

But it first starts with you seeing it for yourself! That's why there's so much power in being in the cocoon by yourself and doing the inner work, and when you come out, you're ready.

> *The cocoon is meant to strengthen your wings for flight, so take your time in isolation!*

Expect Your Byproducts (Effects)

Catalysts are the underlying factors that serve as deep roots, demanding our attention and healing. They are super important because by addressing and excavating these catalysts, we can embark on a journey of healing. However, if left unaddressed, they can give rise to consequential outcomes known as byproducts.

Byproducts are the effects that arise from the experiences we have endured in life. They can be seen as the symptoms that manifest when we start on a profound journey of self-reflection. Exploring these byproducts allows us to gain deeper insights into ourselves and our personal growth.

Acknowledging and embracing the catalysts in our lives requires immense bravery and vulnerability. It entails engaging in self-reflection and nurturing a sincere intention to foster positive change. By embarking on this transformative journey, we open ourselves to personal growth and the discovery of our true selves.

The Power of the Ego

In my generation, there was zero tolerance for bullying or allowing others to perceive us as weak or timid. I was raised with the belief that I must always assert myself with confidence and make it clear that I meant business.

Do not be perceived as a pushover!

And people mistreating or lying to me, or when individuals believed they could escape the consequences of their negative actions. As a result, I would always be ready to defend myself and stand up for the truth.

Being a nurse for over twenty years, I have learned how to be a patient advocate and stand up for what is right. I want to talk to you about how your chosen profession can also impact how you show up in other areas of your life. I had my own revelation in this regard. It was mind-blowing, to say the least!

I can admit that I lived by this code for a long time until I realized how to pick and choose my battles wisely! It is often said that your first impression of someone is everlasting. And that when you choose to overlook certain behaviors, or actions without addressing them, you inadvertently communicate to others how they can treat you and the boundaries you are willing to accept.

Learning that your words have power is imperative to a more peaceful life.

The Bible emphasizes the immense power of our words, urging us to choose them wisely. Words have the potential to bring life or cause harm, so we must be mindful of the impact they can have on others.

Through personal growth and experiences, I've come to realize the value of responding with composure, particularly when faced with challenges to my ego. The ego often acts as a shield, compelling us to react fiercely or seek retribution when provoked.

I've also learned that investing my time and energy into unnecessary conflicts only yields negative outcomes. It is far more productive to prioritize my mental well-being and maintain a sense of inner peace by consciously choosing which battles to engage in. By carefully selecting the situations that truly require a response, I can channel my energy towards more meaningful endeavors. This enables me to preserve my mental stability, reduce stress, and gain a deeper understanding of what truly matters in life. Your end goal is to *Respond versus React* because it leaves you with so much more inner peace within your spirit!

The Struggle of Isolation

There is a common misconception that isolation is a form of punishment, but I challenge that notion. Instead, I believe that at times, we are called to experience periods of separation and solitude for a greater purpose. It is during these times of isolation that we have the opportunity to truly discover our authentic selves and fulfill our unique purpose in life. Rather than viewing isolation as a negative experience, I encourage you to see it as a transformative journey of self-discovery and personal growth.

During my divorce, I experienced a period of isolation and separation from my family and friends. I call it my pruning phase of life! I truly learned who was in my corner and who would no longer be on this journey with me. In hindsight, I am so grateful for my period of isolation because I got to learn who I was without all the mind drama and chaos of life.

> *I also got to learn who Jineen was without all the titles!*

It truly gave me a sense of clarity and inner peace, which helped me discover my purpose in life. God knew what he was doing, it was good that I was afflicted.

At times, being in the company of others can cloud our vision and hinder our ability to see the path that God has set before us. These distractions can steer us off course from fulfilling our purpose. However, it's important to remember that God's perspective surpasses our own limited view.

> *While we can only see up to the corner of the hill, God sees beyond that, with complete knowledge of what lies ahead.*

By shifting our perspective and trusting in His guidance, we can come to understand that isolation is not something happening to us, but rather something designed for our benefit.

It is during a time of separation that allows us to draw closer to God, gain clarity, and align ourselves with His plans. In this understanding, we can embrace isolation as a means of personal growth and alignment with our true purpose.

Isolation can be perceived as a state of not belonging or struggling with acceptance. However, it's important to recognize that belonging is a mindset and a feeling that can be developed regardless of external circumstances. Similarly, acceptance encompasses the same notion. Do you accept and embrace yourself? Do you believe that you belong in your current situation or environment? It all boils down to the lens through which you view life and the outlook you hold. As a mindset coach, I encourage you to shift your mindset towards accepting where you are today and extending grace to yourself in this space. Remember, your self-worth remains constant at 100%, whether you're experiencing success or learning from setbacks.

From observing animals, (bear with me for a moment) both in their mating habits and their approach to life, I believe there are valuable lessons to be learned. For example, eagles are very impressive and intriguing animals. They do not feed on dead things, only live prey! In their instinctual wisdom, these birds let go of things that no longer serve or benefit them. They soar to great heights, flying alone yet not feeling lonely, as they do not depend on a flock to elevate them. Eagles also fly above turbulent clouds. They get the wind underneath their wings to soar above storm clouds by riding the storm out with ease.

It is empowering to embrace the truth that during life's challenges and storms, it is okay to find solace in solitude, to rise above the storm clouds, and to hold onto the assurance that every storm eventually passes. Eventually, you may have to build a new tribe when exiting a period of isolation. Remember it is a critical piece of your healing and self-discovery journey.

> *Bloom where you are in your Intentional Queen Journey! Believe in yourself! Love yourself on the deepest level!*

Just like plants, sometimes you may need to be relocated to a more fertile environment or surrounded by better conditions in order to thrive and grow. This is one reason why I love the lotus flower because it comes up through the murky water to shine up beautifully every time.

Remind yourself at times that the people you surround yourself with have a significant influence on your personal growth and manifestation. Therefore, it is crucial to assess and choose wisely the individuals you spend the most time with, particularly as you embark on your journey of manifesting and entering a new season of life.

> *You become like the five people you spend the most time with daily!*

Boundaries and Triggers

If you often find yourself being a people pleaser, it's likely that you struggle with setting healthy and firm boundaries in your relationships. This struggle is remarkably common, especially among women. Remember that boundaries are for you to have safe guardrails around your precious self. They are parameters you give yourself of how you want to interact with people, places, and things. Sometimes, they're even in your parenting role! These kids will try you in these streets to see what they can get away with! My son is the Prince of Negotiation! I wonder where he gets it from? Probably me!

But honestly, take some time for some self-reflection on the things you need in certain moments, so that way you know when to reinforce a boundary. Also, I encourage you to sit with yourself and analyze what makes you feel peaceful within your body. This is usually a sign that you have properly set a healthy boundary.

Teach people how to treat you.

Most of the time people struggle with reinforcing boundaries because they don't like to cause friction or have people mad at them. They can be perceived as easygoing and passive. But as time progresses, you'll gradually understand that people will become accustomed to this pattern and may exploit your willingness to their own advantage, resulting in harm to yourself. This is when you feel overwhelmed, stretched too thin, and begin neglecting yourself.

Take heed that this can be in your personal and professional life! To avoid this detriment to your well-being, it is important to understand your own capacity and ability to show up for people, but most importantly yourself! The wonderful thing about setting boundaries for yourself is that you are teaching your children how to do this too, and hopefully, it will be a lot easier for them if they witness and understand it from a young age.

Once you create healthy boundaries, make sure to adhere to the consequences you have set in place with the people who violate them. We teach people how to treat us by what we allow them to do when it comes to us mentally, physically, and spiritually.

The perfect example is in the scenario of airline safety whereby it is crucial to attend to your own needs by applying your own oxygen mask before helping others around you. Let go of the enabling spirit of overextending for people to the detriment of yourself.

You have to teach them how to fish, so they will never go hungry!

I even do this in my parenting style with my son. It is called letting go of carrying everyone else's weight, responsibilities, and duties that they can do for themselves. Your load will become lighter, while your capacity will increase, and at the same time, you're giving them the gift of independence that they will most certainly need in the years to come.

You will also feel more productive, energetic, and peaceful, and overall alleviate the overwhelm of these burdens. This will allow you to function at the highest level of yourself, and believe me, it's a wonderful feeling.

Create healthy boundaries and identify your triggers!

Triggers will negatively ignite an emotional response in your body during certain situations, which usually leads to anger or discord. And triggers can happen lightning fast! But by identifying your triggers, you have more control over how you respond when you are in those uncomfortable situations.

"Calmness is mastery!"- James Allen

Responding calmly versus reacting is a key indicator that you have now controlled your triggers, instead of them controlling you.

This was one of the biggest hurdles to overcome in my own self-discovery and transformative journey, and it took time and effort and of course. I had my setbacks. But it gets easier!

People-pleasing Tendencies

When you have people-pleasing tendencies it can result in dishonoring yourself. It really can. You lack the ability to truly show up as your authentic self to the detriment of stretching yourself too thin and lacking self-love. Shrinking to make others feel better can lead to resentment and bitterness over time.

Be vigilant and mindful of how you operate when interacting with others!

People pleasing can be a slippery slope, especially if it resembles duties that you perform in your professional life. Let's take the nursing career as an example. Nurses are trained caregivers, which usually means that the patient comes first. Even before you can take a break or use the bathroom! Over time, this creates an innate pattern to start putting everyone else's needs ahead of your own needs. This leads to overwhelm and self-neglect if not managed properly. In the United States, there is a significant rise in burnout and a growing number of nurses leaving the workforce. I strongly believe that this is connected to the lack of essential elements of mindfulness and self-care, and the pushing of nurses to their limit and beyond.

There's only so much one person can handle, and the overwhelm can therefore spill over into your personal life with family and motherhood because everyone needs to get fulfilled before you! If only there were three of us! But the fact is, we are just one woman trying to juggle many things. Something has to give. And that is why I encourage you to shift your mindset to taking care of yourself, (putting your safety mask on first before putting your child's on), you can better serve and show up for everyone else! This was a huge mindset shift that changed the trajectory of how I show up in my personal and professional life.

You are important and your needs matter too!

Throughout my 23-year journey as a nurse, with ten of those years as an Advanced Practice Registered Nurse, I have experienced tremendous challenges and personal growth. The path to success required immense dedication, perseverance, and sacrifices. Along the way, I have earned accolades and titles that signify my accomplishments. You know me, I want to do my best! I also faced adversity and jealousy along the way from those who were resistant to my intentions of breaking molds and charting my own course. Being a woman of color and having high aspirations at a young age caused me to be on this people-pleasing slippery slope! Diversity, equity, and inclusion are barriers that most ambitious women face in their professional careers.

From an early stage in my professional career, I found myself navigating the need to code-switch and adapt to fit in with others. I felt the pressure to shrink myself in certain situations to make others feel more at ease in my presence. Unfortunately, this also led to a reluctance to fully celebrate my accomplishments, fearing that I would be perceived as bragging. This overall behavior began to pose a challenge as it delved into my experience of seeking approval and striving to maintain a successful career alongside a fulfilling home life. I was just so tired of being in that vicious cycle of pushing myself to the maximum and not recognizing my capacity! I didn't want that guilt or shame either that we all commonly face in our lives! However, life has a way of intervening and forcing us to slow down. The pandemic, in particular, impacted everyone and prompted reflection on the importance of creating a balanced life. It was at this juncture that I reached a crossroads and realized the necessity of embracing a season of softness and self-care. Also, I began to incorporate more self-love and compassion for myself! And it was wonderful.

Perfection Paralysis

Perfection paralysis is a challenge I've faced since my youth, particularly during my pursuit of academic excellence as valedictorian. I now realize it is such self-sabotaging behavior. It can hinder your ability to experience true joy and contentment with life. With the moments right in front of you. It can sometimes prevent you from moving forward, remaining stuck on a hamster wheel of overwhelm and stress!

I have even seen it cause increased isolation and lack of connection with others. Remember that no one is perfect, and the goal is to strive for excellence, not necessarily perfection.

I have found so much freedom in letting go of perfectionism. It is a sneaky thing, so I encourage you to be mindful when you feel its presence! Now, I show up to the best of my ability but with integrity and pivot if things don't turn out the way I planned. You must hold onto the idea of knowing that you are enough today, and you are enough tomorrow.

The journey is not linear but with peaks and valleys of life!

Give yourself grace in this space, especially when performing new tasks. Don't become stuck because you're not sure or have doubts. I believe that when you start to take the baby step over time, your courage will grow. You will shed perfectionism because you will realize that you can now let in vulnerability and people will come to respect you more. People will relate to you more! No one can relate to a perfectionist! They understand that you make mistakes as well. And often the beautiful thing is once people see you are fallible too, they are more likely to share their own struggles, enabling your relationship to become closer as you bond further.

The goal is understanding how you deal with your blunders in life and recognizing that everybody has their own struggles, so you are not alone in that journey. It all starts with your thoughts on why you feel it needs to be that way. But you can come to a point in your life where you say, *"That's good enough"*. Better yet, *"I gave it my best shot"*. You always can try the next day to show up better than the day before, with God by your side. Practicing over time will lead you to be able to do something fluently, confidently, and consistently. As a mother, I encourage this mindset shift with my son at school or when he's trying a new skill. I emphasize the importance of consistent practice, highlighting that repetition and perseverance over time result in noticeable improvement. The goal is not to quit unless you've hit a point of insanity! Then, yes, it's time for a break!

I mean, insanity is doing something over and over expecting a different result. However, when you have progressed over perfection then you know that you are moving in the right direction. *Let it go, let it flow!*

> **Show up for yourself and the people who need you!**

Imposter Syndrome

Imposter Syndrome has so many layers to it in my opinion because it can encompass many parts of your life: relationships, work, self-worth, self-love, your value, and/or motherhood. This term can be defined as thinking you are not worthy or good enough in some area of your life. The reality is that you are always exactly where you are right now! We all can use some fine-tuning or self-improvement, and that's fine, but please know (from the bottom of my heart!) that your value doesn't change if you're winning or losing. You will always be complete and whole!

I included the word "restoration" in my podcast title for this reason because it is a journey to become a whole version of yourself. I wanted the end goal to be that women are empowered to become whole in their being and truly love themselves to the highest level possible. But not that you cannot love anyone fully until you love yourself fully. Self-love is termed a cliche at times, and we all know this stuff, but do we really know it? It is so key for your core well-being, and it makes you a better version of yourself when you recognize it. When you emanate self-love, it will help you in other relationships in your life, even with your kids!

I want to offer you some time to reflect on this section. For example, get a journal or piece of paper right now. Stop…I will wait for you lol! Now, first I want you to write down ten self-affirming statements, and make sure you start them as an "I am" statement. For example, "I am a good person," or "I am proud of what I've achieved so far".

Now that you've written down your ten affirmations, I want you to read them aloud at least two-three times a day for the next three weeks! Why? Well, it takes an estimated 21 days to learn a new behavior. And the reason must say them aloud is so you can pivot your subconscious mind into believing these positive seeds you are sowing into your mind. Did you think I wasn't going to coach you on self-love, self-healing, and a growth mindset? You are officially a part of the Intentional Queen Journey Tribe now, and I strongly believe iron sharpens iron! Transform your self-perception by embracing this suggestion on your journey of personal growth. Note that my suggestions are rooted in my own experiences and the strategies that have helped me on my path of self-improvement. So, these are just a guide. Now is all about you! Your thoughts and your positive seeds that you will sow in your mind. So, rework it where necessary, trust your instinct and go with what feels right for you. Ultimately, these thoughts will lead to how you feel about yourself, including your self-love, self-worth, and value!

Self-Worth and Confidence

Knowing your value and having self-belief are important things to reflect upon in your transformative and self-discovery journey. Begin by digging a little deeper, loving, and believing in yourself with a new, fresh, and nurturing change in your perspective. Sometimes, we can have a distorted view of ourselves. Thinking that we are not enough or living in shame and guilt! I am here to tell you that you are enough, right here and in your future! We can get it so misconstrued that we wrap ourselves up in our titles!

But who are you really? For you certainly are not simply what you do. That is the more valuable question that I want you to explore. If you don't know where to start, read Proverbs 31 in the Bible. Figure out who God says you are. Once you learn who you are and you understand what you do, it allows you to identify the difference. How do you become confident?

By being courageous and showing up for yourself daily! Imagine a flower that blooms in the springtime.

As you continue to show up daily, your confidence will skyrocket! Believing in yourself that you can do this, that you are enough, will become a learned behavior before you know it.

I encourage you to also evaluate your intentions of why you desire certain things in life. These will become your purpose, the reason why you're doing what you're doing on your personal discovery journey to wholeness.

I want to emphasize the importance of not relying solely on others' opinions and expectations when setting your intentions. Doing so can potentially lead to feelings of resentment or bitterness if things don't unfold as anticipated.

As I received recognition from others for the multitude of accomplishments and milestones I have achieved, it brought to my attention the profound significance of my own journey. It became clear that God has instilled in me a purpose, a divine "Why". It became my personal obligation and duty to walk in obedience and fulfill it. Sometimes, He provides us with a blueprint, a set of tasks we must undertake in order to reach the destination He has intended for us. It all boils down to showing up for the one individual who needs you the most at that time. If more people are impacted, that is considered a bonus in my bonus!

I have come to understand that my faithfulness lies in simply showing up, taking action, and remaining steadfast in my commitment. This unwavering dedication has led me to accumulate numerous "receipts," tangible proof of my efforts and achievements, serving as a testament to the faith and determination I possess. I love being a Woman of Faith, mother, mindset coach, and whatever else God decides to lay in my path! I have grown more appreciation for the little things and staying in a space of gratitude!

CHAPTER 4

Shape the Outcome

Digging Deeper

As a mindset coach, I empower you to dig even a little deeper now, into your personal beliefs, so we can shape your outcome of living a more fulfilled life.

I recall watching Disney's "The Princess and the Frog" and being captivated by a song on the soundtrack titled "Dig a Little Deeper." It resonated with me as the princess in the movie, a diligent worker, realized the importance of slowing down and digging deeper to understand her own needs and desires.

Now, keep in mind there is a difference between what you need and what you want! I believe in my life there were so many things that I wanted but it's not necessarily what I needed. When you take the time for some self-reflection and embrace self-acceptance, you gain the ability to assess your current situation and discern the next steps on your path.

By acknowledging the catalysts and byproducts that have influenced your journey and desire to elevate your outcomes, you are taking steps towards becoming a better, upgraded version of yourself. You are now aware, and there's no looking back!

Reclaiming Wholeness

Heal and come to a place of complete love for yourself!

Reclaiming wholeness within yourself resembles knowing your self-worth and giving yourself grace in this space while you are embarking on your transformative personal journey. It will serve you as you continue on your own Intentional Queen Journey! *Replace the bad seeds with good seeds.* Check in with the thoughts that you ruminate on a daily basis. This is why I believe journaling is so powerful. It allows you to release the clutter in your mind and reflect on the things that were bothering you at the time. Go back to those broken places and heal them one at a time! Remember that *healed people can heal people!* Be okay with being different and the change agent. Feed your mind every day with something that's going to nourish and empower your spirit. Talk to yourself in a positive manner whether that be through journaling or affirmations. Cast down negative thoughts that no longer serve you! Your thoughts lead to feelings, which means that your actions are soon to follow. Thoughts have power and usually, wherever the mind goes the body goes too.

Trusting the Process

Embrace the unknown and have the courage to undergo a transformation, even when it feels daunting. Trusting the process is essential for unlocking your full potential and experiencing remarkable growth.

Become comfortable with being uncomfortable!

This is a fundamental affirmation that I give my clients when we first start working together because it's so important to realize that you will have to stretch yourself outside of your comfort zone. Remember that a rubber band is not working at its full capacity unless it is being stretched. When the rubber band is not in tension, it is not holding onto anything. Life always changes anyway, whether we hold on tightly or not, so it's best to bend, stretch and go with the flow and see what happens!

Consider whether your actions will ignite a transformative journey within you, allowing you to navigate your personal Crossroads with resilience and purpose. The goal is to cultivate clarity, restore confidence, and embrace wholeness as you enter your next season of life. Pearls and diamonds are made by experiencing pressure to become beautiful gems!

> *Remember they are valuable treasures, and so are you!*

Embrace the power of knowing your self-worth and the value that you possess. Again, I'm reminded of the beautiful meaning of lotus flowers, how they go through the murky water to show up bright and beautiful. They are known for their beauty and resilience! You too can be like the lotus, embracing the dirt and darkness of the journey allowing you to rise and become the person you're meant to be, even if it's not what you initially expected. Acceptance of the trials and tribulations in life allows you to elevate your thinking and begin to shift your perspective on your transformative journey to restoration. *Trust the process!*

Renewing of Your Mindset

Throughout Bible scripture, there is an emphasis on the transformative power of renewing your mind, highlighting its essential importance in personal growth and development. The thoughts we dwell upon in our minds have the power to influence our mental well-being, potentially leading to anxiety, depression, or other emotional struggles. We don't need to just accept these thoughts. We can challenge them to see if they are serving us well. We can renew them if they are not.

Many people struggle in silence through mental issues because they don't feel comfortable speaking up or getting the help that they need. I am not a therapist, but I can speak from personal experience! You must heal the past so you can catapult yourself forward. Life coaching is the notion of taking the remnants from your healing journey and moving forward to live a more fulfilled life on your own terms. As your mindset coach, my role is to guide and support you on your journey toward your desired finish line, while helping you incorporate more self-love in the process. Together, we will walk hand in hand, with me as your accountability partner, reminding you that you have the ability to achieve your goals because I have walked the same path myself.

When you burst out of the cocoon too soon, your wings will not be strengthened enough by the tension that's within the cocoon walls. This premature exit will prevent you from having the ability to fly on your own.

Now, be careful of the enabling spirit! The desire to help people all the time can be unhelpful. It is better to teach people how to be capable of doing some of these tasks themselves. So, I propose you teach people how to be independent or interdependent within their capacity level. Holding people accountable but also instructing them how to do it themselves because it will be forever lasting. I believe that this concept can be applied in motherhood as well!

"Train up a child in the way they should go!" - Proverbs 22:6 NKJV

Just as mother eagles push their young birds out of the nest and make it uncomfortable, it serves as a reminder that growth requires stepping out of our comfort zones. It's a natural process of learning to fly, with the mother eagle providing guidance and support without doing it for them. Are you ready to embrace a mindset shift and soar to new heights?

Becoming Coachable

Becoming coachable allows for the acceleration of your personal growth and success. This is the key to unlocking your true potential. Embracing coachability means being open-minded and receptive to guidance, actively seeking opportunities for growth, and demonstrating a willingness to learn. Till this day, I still have a coach and therapist to keep me on track to progressing in certain areas of my personal and professional development. Being coachable has allowed me to be a better mindset coach, mother, friend, and family member. When you seek the nurturement and support of others, it is called making an investment in yourself. It involves being humble enough to accept feedback, taking the initiative to apply new insights, and remaining committed to personal development. Being coachable allows you to tap into the wisdom and expertise of others, leveraging their guidance to enhance your performance and make meaningful progress. It allows you to identify blind spots, break through limitations, and adopt a growth mindset.

Embarking on my personal journey has revealed my true calling as a mindset coach, dedicated to transforming the minds of women and guiding them on their path toward wholeness and self-improvement. Through my own experiences, I've gained the insight and passion to support others in leveling up to become the best versions of themselves. It's a rewarding endeavor that allows me to empower women, helping them unlock their true potential and embrace a life of growth and fulfillment.

I have come to believe that the lessons and mistakes I've experienced were divine interventions, guiding me towards my true purpose in life. It is as if God, in His wisdom, molded and shaped me according to His vision, leading me on a unique journey to reach this significant point.

Never forget and feel comforted by the fact that sometimes we stumble upon unexpected paths because God has already ordained our destinies, and it is through these twists and turns that we ultimately arrive at our destined crossroads.

> *"You're the average of the five people you spend the most time with."- Jim Rohn*

So, choose wisely while you are developing into a better version of yourself.

> *"Your network is your net worth." - Tim Sanders*

Stay around people with integrity and who are on the same trajectory of personal growth.

> *Baby steps lead to giant leaps!*

It wasn't until I recognized the impact of sharing my voice on the podcast three years ago that I realized I was becoming a beacon of hope for those lost in the darkness, providing them a safe haven to find their own path. I must admit, that reaching out to others can be challenging at times, as it may stir up memories and triggers from my own journey. Nonetheless, I understand the importance of extending a helping hand, for I will never forget the trials I've overcome, and being on the other side, seeing how wonderful it is, makes me want to help others get there, too.

Harriet Tubman serves as a powerful example of going back to rescue slaves, even after achieving her own freedom. It's not an obligation, but rather a heartfelt desire to ensure others don't remain trapped, bound, or lost on their own. I strive to help others break free from their conflicts and limitations, guiding them toward a path of growth, empowerment, and self-discovery!

PART TWO
BE INTENTIONAL

CHAPTER 5

Give Yourself Permission to Slow Down

First, let's define being intentional. Merriam-Webster's definition of intentional means *done by intent or design.* People use the word very loosely. However, I really took this word into my heart and spirit. Hence, I named my business with this word in it. I wanted to do all things with positive intentions and with being obedient in my life choices and of which God has in plan for my life!

Now, having intentionality and living a life of purpose required me to give myself permission to slow down. I had to slow down from over-exerting myself in my day-to-day life. I knew it was affecting my health and relationships. But finally, this slowing down began, and it all started with a deliberate thought of giving myself grace, but also recognizing the difference between God's and society's viewpoints on intentionality. Let's break this down a little further.

> *"But seek ye first the kingdom of God, and his righteousness; and all these things shall be added unto you." - Matthew 6:33 KJV*

God wants us to live a life of good intentions but walk in our purpose and gifts. This in turn will give us the dream life that we desire when we seek him as our source. I have grown to use this scripture to help me delineate what way I am operating in life in my pursuit of success.

So, society's viewpoint on intentionality tends to push the agenda of grind hard no matter the cost. I have had that mindset when I was in survival mode, but to my detriment, it cost me valuable time, energy, my well-being, and more! As I mentioned, I became ill with my thyroid disease, my marriage ended, and I hit my rock bottom! I had really just lost myself in the chaos of life!

But I no longer dwell in those places because of the power of grace. Survival mode no longer served me like it did in recent years.

The Releasing of Superwoman Syndrome

Remember our childhood female superheroes like Wonder Woman? She had superpowers and could do it all with her mask and cape intact. Hence the term Superwoman Syndrome, suggesting that you are a woman who can do it all without breaking down. Superwoman Syndrome manifests when the weight of responsibility compels you to take on multiple roles and fulfill everyone's needs, often at the expense of your own well-being. This can potentially lead to losing yourself in the process, and it so often has sadly led so many women before us to lose themselves.

Society does have a pretty set-in stigma and pressure surrounding the myth that mothers are able (and should be able) to do it all; take care of family, work full-time, cook, clean, and anything else that falls under homemaking. Most moms carry the full mental load of running a household. It can be an extreme challenge and a daunting feat, which leads to self-neglect and overwhelm! Caregivers tend to fall into this pattern, constantly giving without replenishing their own energy reserves. It is important to give from your overflow and not from a diluted version of yourself.

My mom is a very ambitious woman who instilled in me to always keep pressing and do whatever I needed to do in order to care for my family. I remember my parents working multiple jobs while also seeking higher education when my siblings and I were young. To me, it was normal to grind! My parents used to say, "Pay me now or Pay me later"! What they were trying to tell us was do we want to work hard in our younger years or in our older years of life? Most people look at retirement as a time to slow down, so in my mind, I took this as good advice and wanted to grind out my 20's and 30's to set myself up for a more comfortable retirement period later in life. This all made perfect sense in my mind, but sometimes my body let me know it was pushed to the max.

When I was in nurse anesthesia school, I had to go on a home heart monitor for a couple of weeks. I was having heart palpitations and dizziness spells, so I had to be rushed to the emergency room. It turned out that I was having these symptoms due to lack of rest combined with increased caffeine intake, and high levels of chronic stress. It was a wake-up call to me that my body was sending me alerts to slow down, but I was too focused on my pursuit of success to even listen.

However, I now know that becoming intentional about prioritizing your self-care and mental health is vital to maintaining your inner peace. Please don't leave it to the point where you're having horrible and even life-threatening symptoms. Move yourself into a space of gratitude and give yourself permission to slow down!

Check in with your body, mind, and soul on a routine basis!

This will allow you to quiet your body and recognize all the things it is trying to tell you that need improvement. That needs rest. I mean, think of it like this. We take our vehicles for routine maintenance and when the check engine light comes on, we are right onto it! Think of the body in the same manner. Actually no, think of it as a much more important thing than your car! Begin to prioritize health and your own needs before providing care for others.

Self-care and self-love are not selfish!

We forget that we are not actually helpful to others around us if we are not our best selves, if we are worn out! So, in order to be able to help and nurture others, we just have to nurture ourselves. I need to adopt these mindset shifts in all areas of my life! And when we fall into an old unhelpful pattern, we just forgive ourselves and bring ourselves back.

In my coaching experience, I've noticed from time to time some women can use the idea of being there for everyone but themselves, as a crutch in life. These women don't allow anyone else to step in to help them because they lack trust and want things to be perfect. To be done their way. I would even go further to say it can be related to a lack of healthy boundaries and wanting to keep everyone happy (people-pleasing). You could go even further in some circumstances whereby some people choose to focus on everyone else because they are avoiding facing difficult decisions or are scared to make changes to make themselves happy. What if they fail? They can use the excuse of having no time in order to avoid facing some hard truths.

But back to the problem with trying to be perfect. You can lack true authenticity and vulnerability to be yourself. This then leads to resentment, guilt, shame, and eventually burnout! That's why I empower you to become better, and not bitter. It's time to give yourself permission to experience these fleeting feelings but make a deadline for when you will release them. All the while, give yourself grace because it can be very challenging. Allow yourself to have setbacks.

> *Your intentional thoughts that you marinate in will, if not now, show up at some point in other ways with your mood and feelings about things going on in your life.*

And what happens next, is your feelings and actions are soon to follow, and that's when we might behave in ways we may regret. So, are you with me? Let's cast down negative thoughts and replace them with positive self-talk because now you are functioning with preferable actions that serve you in your own journey!

How to Bounce Back after Burnout

We know that struggling with burnout from spreading yourself too thin in your daily life can become detrimental to your overall health. On my own journey to bounce back from burnout, I realized the importance of proactive self-care versus reactive self-care.

Reactive self-care happens when you are forced to slow down for whatever reason, and you can no longer operate at full capacity. I started to have health problems with my weight, blood pressure, and thyroid. These red indicators were my body's way of saying I was actually in burnout mode and my body was shutting down. Proactive self-care is not letting yourself get to that point! It is paying attention to your body's signals, realizing that your cup is getting low, that your capacity has hit its high, and doing something to refill yourself in real-time versus after the fact. Even being proactive before this level is ideal.

I envision looking at my vehicle's oil change sticker, knowing when my car service is coming up. Now, I have two decisions to make. Get the car serviced when it is due or wait until my car breaks down from lack of service! My parents always told me it is easier to maintain something than try to fix it once it is broken. There is so much truth in that statement, which can apply to multiple areas in your life!

Make sure to check in with yourself and your needs routinely. So, how do you change your capacity when there's so much to do? That's the million-dollar question. Sometimes its letting things go or maybe it is being present in the moment, realizing that the future has not happened yet. It might be focusing simply on what is in front of you at that moment and not getting too far ahead of yourself. It could be cutting back on something that doesn't help you – such as too much social media that sucks your time. Or spending time with people who are not worth your time. It's about controlling the things that you can control. Better yet, allowing people to do their roles and play their part. Hold people accountable! Delegate! As a recovering people pleaser, this truly was a heavy one for me to acknowledge and put into practice. But the above key things catapulted my mental wellness and activated my mindfulness with more of a life of ease.

Seek your support team to offload some of your responsibilities, you are not an island of one person! Let go of perfection or of telling yourself you need to do it all and allow people to help you and take over some of the overflow. No one wants a martyr. They want a person to connect with, to share life with. And that's why I coach my clients to realize that their family is good when you are good. So, don't put it off any longer, till you're broken down like and car that was forgotten to be serviced. Make yourself a priority because your family will thank you in the end, plus it will decrease your mommy guilt and overwhelm.

Take some time out to sit down and work this thing out. Get a list happening of what needs to be done, what can be delegated and what can be let go. When I was overwhelmed trying to manage being a wife, mother, and highly-stressed health professional, I struggled to try to do all the things I wanted to do. I really wanted to have my house cleaned professionally to take another task off my plate and give me more time to focus on other things. Because I had made up my mind on this one, the universe made it happen. When people asked what I needed, I said a professional cleaning service. And you know what? My request honored by my mother for a Christmas gift. My house was cleaned to my standards, and I was less stressed too! The perfect gift! More than anything, my professional housekeeper became a great friend from our first encounter and beyond! God has a way of bringing people into your life for a reason and a season. I will forever be grateful for that divine connection!

We've discussed the importance of boundaries. Now, while you're resetting after burnout (or near burnout) is the time for perhaps establishing healthy boundaries or adjusting boundaries to be healthier. Be sure about them before asking for help from others or delegating tasks. Remember, boundaries are for you to maintain your security within yourself. But you must know your capacity and stick with it. Don't forget that "no" is a complete sentence that does not require an explanation from anyone. If someone disrespects or continues to challenge your boundaries, it is time for you to take action that best serves you.

Reevaluate your inner circle. Who is really there for you? And who is not? Pruning accordingly! I strongly believe that some relationships have an expiration date. It's not easy. But we need to be okay with losing people in life or in love. We have one life and limited hours in each day. You absolutely should not be including people in your life who are toxic or hold you down. We can understand that some people may not be stepping into your next season or chapter of life with you. They were there for a season, and that season has ended. During my own pruning process, I lost relationships with people that I thought would be coming with me into my next chapter of life. For example, when my divorce happened, it was devastating to say the least. I had lost a major person in my life. I had to embrace the fact that I was going to become a single mother, which was so hard for me to accept because of the stigma of single motherhood. I am grateful that I am healing through that chapter of my life and living in a space of acceptance at the end of the marriage. To be honest, I learned to never lose myself again after all I endured. I also learned how to love myself on a deeper level, which is why I am a self-love expert.

Address your health concerns. If you neglect to, they could evolve into life-threatening issues. I went on a mission to take better care of myself, physically as well as mentally. I signed up for kickboxing and got myself a personal trainer. Go me! My personal trainer was an ambitious mom as well, and she helped me lose thirty pounds. This also improved my self-confidence. For most of my life I struggled with my weight, but this time I felt my comeback was personal and I was determined to give the training program my all. I believe investing in yourself in whatever capacity you have will help you grow from the inside out. This is just part of my physical transformation, but one year later, I had turned every health problem around! Healed and blessed!

I want to express the importance here on this journey, of seeking God for yourself. There's nothing like learning from him and trusting him to help you handle situations that you didn't even know he could tap into and help you with. Get yourself a few foundational scriptures that you can refer to on a routine basis to keep you empowered during the course of your journey. These will become focal reference points for you to maintain intentional positive thoughts and cast down negative thoughts. Place them on your mirror, phone as a screensaver, or somewhere you can see them regularly. Review them frequently, ideally on a daily basis to make them a learned habit!

> *Change your mindset from you doing everything of your own free will to doing things with Christ who strengthens you! Trust the process!*

CHAPTER 6

Own Your Role and Take Accountability

Becoming more self-aware and giving myself permission to slow down was a pivotal moment in my life. It doesn't stop there though! This only begins the transformation of doing the inner work or being in the cocoon. The cocoon phase takes the longest and can be a daunting feat when in isolation. However, growth is done in motion.

> *Own your role in the situation by becoming accountable!*

Creating balance can be challenging for ambitious women, trying to do all the so many things with excellence. At some point, some things will begin to slip through the cracks and potentially break. That's when it's time to acknowledge you are hitting rock bottom! But most importantly, you need to do something about it! And you need to want to do something about it. Realizing these cardinal steps will begin to move you forward and put you in a better position intentionally for your next season. Level up to the better version of yourself!

> *"Faith without works is dead" - James 2:14-26 ESV*

Let's unpack what has happened in your life, develop some discipline, and become courageous to embark on the inner work at hand. Honestly, I believe that there could be a team of people assisting in this special process such as God, a life coach, and a therapist! However, you have to be ready to be vulnerable to share your own story and to accept you need help.

Working through the pandemic as a certified registered nurse anesthetist and newfound life coach, while still trying to balance the other areas of my life was exhausting! I was in constant pursuit of success, but I was simply living in survival mode the whole time. I lost precious time with my family, and worrying about my own safety took its toll on me. I was definitely not leading a life of ease! I was overwhelmed and neglecting myself. Not to mention feeling guilty and resentful that I was suffering in silence! Compassion fatigue was everywhere around me. People (me included) were exhausted from witnessing so much suffering, dying, and sadness all around them. Sadly, I personally knew a few people who had committed suicide or were struggling with mental health issues from experiencing these things. Honestly, I believe it does do something to your psyche and your mind. There's only so much that people can take.

> **I purposefully made the decision to prioritize myself more and help people too!**

And as I said, for me personally (and yours might be very different), this looked like - getting a personal trainer, setting healthier boundaries, getting a therapist, and ultimately, just sharing my story! As I began to prioritize myself and think of a strategy to help me become better holistically, I realized I was taking accountability for some of my misconceptions and limited beliefs. This led to a change in my perspective and a shift in my mindset. I continued to develop myself because I felt it was important to put myself first so that I could be the best person for everyone in my life!

I had declared that self-care and self-love were non-negotiables in my life. I became the Queen of Love as my friends and clients called me. In turn, it helped me be a better mother and person overall. I blocked out time for myself and recognized when I was becoming too overwhelmed, and I could see the rationale behind it. I tackled those catalysts and began seeing different by-products. In other words, I was able to see the fruits of my labor. To be honest, it sure did feel like childbirth and labor! It is a painful process, but so rewarding in the biggest scheme of things.

I'll repeat this again because it's just so key - when you are feeling better, then everyone around you will feel better too because you are now refueled and functioning at your best capacity. Remember to believe in yourself!

CHAPTER 7

Self-Love is Not Selfish - Self-Love and Self-Belief

Believe in Yourself

> *"A second is equally important: 'love your neighbor as yourself'." -*
> *Matthew 22:39 NLT*

Loving yourself is a term used often. I want to debunk this for you as a Self-Love Expert. You truly cannot love others until you love yourself. Yes, you've heard it all before, but it is is so true. You will love others through your tainted rose-colored glasses and limited belief systems. The goal is to begin your journey knowing that you want to pivot towards peace and begin feeling safe during your transformation journey! But first, you have to believe in yourself and know you are worthy of healthy love.

> *You are worthy of healthy love!*

That's why I believe that your own test can become testimonies for other people because you can become a framework or a blueprint for them to see the steps ahead. There is power in your self-belief and being intentional about those things because your mindset blooms. What you input in your mind routinely (all those daily thoughts) is what you begin to manifest outwardly. So, if you constantly have bad thoughts then in turn you may manifest bad actions or outcomes in your life. To combat this, I always encourage my clients to talk about positive things, to talk positively to themselves and to repeat daily affirmations. Also, have compassion and grace for yourself during this transition.

Through my own healing journey, I have been able to help thousands of women through my podcast by believing in myself and giving people hope while on their own transformation journeys. Sometimes, I am amazed by my impact, and it can be challenging at times, too. But then someone will send me an email or direct message to tell me that my vulnerability is helping them, so I keep going. I show up for myself daily. Also, I show up for the one person who may need my message. In turn, when you are showing up for yourself, it gives people the opportunity and inspiration to realize that they too can show up for themselves, too! They can also be present in the moment and be intentional.

Self-Worth and Identity

You are enough today and in your future. Your self-worth is crucial because it shows people what you think about yourself and the behavior you will accept from others. It's huge! I mean, we all have insecurities, but amazing things happen if you can learn to be courageous and know that your self-worth is not dictated by the things that you do versus who you are. This means getting clear on knowing that your titles do not define you and becoming a Proverbs 31 woman as in the Bible.

I remember when my marriage was coming to an end. I had felt nervous about the stigma I was going to receive now that I was getting divorced and being a woman of faith. It left me feeling torn and sad because this is not how I wanted my life to turn out. It definitely wasn't what I had envisioned for myself as an ambitious mom at that stage of life with a toddler in tow. I began to think about now I will have to handle most of the financial and physical demands of parenthood by myself related to our custody challenges. I had to also deal with the fact I had friends and family disown me for making the choice to leave a toxic marriage. I am not here to say bad things about my ex-husband. However, it was not a healthy situation for all parties involved, including the children. I remember crying a lot and thinking separation was not fair to my child. However, in hindsight, it was the best choice I made at that time to end my marriage after trying everything I could to keep it together. Remember, insanity is doing the same thing over expecting a different result. Nothing was changing! But after the divorce, my life and confidence have skyrocketed. I feel I am no longer in survival mode. And my son, well, I see him bloom more and more every day.

I have forgiven the people who hurt me because I no longer wanted to feel bitter. I stand by my choice, I stand proudly in my shoes, and I wear single motherhood as a badge versus allowing society to define me. Society does not portray single moms as ambitious, successful, and intelligent. God has continuously showed up for me through my obedient faith walk and sometimes he carried me in my season of isolation. However, he has let me know that he is preparing something far better than me and it was a life lesson.

This also leads me back to boundaries and resentment and all the things we talked about previously because you can wrap yourself up in titles and the things you do for people and lose yourself somewhere in there when those titles are no longer in effect. Your self-worth is always 100 percent whether you're winning or learning. This means you are complete and whole, not fractured nor broken. I think it became easier for me to understand that failure is normal and to look at it from the lens of it being a lesson to be learned by pivoting, and to always keep going. Remembering that life is not perfect, and no one is perfect was a turning point of acceptance for me. Learning to love myself on a deeper level and understanding that as long as I know I am genuinely being intentional about loving myself and showing up for myself, I will exude this to others.

No More Suffering in Silence

After I really got to know my worth and what I brought to the table, I began to become more vulnerable and have some meekness in the storm. "Meekness in the Storm" was the title of my first podcast episode, which was all about how we can have humility during life challenges while doing it with grace. It was when I decided that I was ready to share my story and no longer suffer in silence. I knew there were women far beyond my physical reach who needed me and wanted community just as much as I did. So, from that point on, I used my platform to help others break free too! I wanted to help all women on their journeys to restoration. The proof was in them sending me their breakthroughs and testimonies! I was so happy for them and so grateful!

During my time of reflection, I recognized that my mom's initial years of single motherhood were things that I was trying to escape in my own motherhood journey. However, I began to see some true similarities things in our stories. I didn't want her previous struggles and more than anything, I didn't want to disappoint her. This was my purpose and goal to break this generational cycle, and I see that clearly now. My mother and I have had candid conversations, and truth be told, it turned out, I freed her too! You don't know how much that warms my heart to hear that as a daughter! My parents never doubted my decision to get divorced and have still always been my biggest support team while I navigated my newfound journey of intentionality. On top of that, they were so proud of me once they listened to my podcast. They proudly shared it with people they knew could benefit from my messages.

Being humble is a big thing when you decide to leave survival mode and no longer suffer in silence. Humility is hard because to humble yourself means being in a state of meekness and vulnerability. This was a pivotal moment in my own self-love journey. You deserve it as well, so don't be afraid to share your story to help others overcome what you have been through!

Seek Wise Counsel

It is so important to be intentional with the positive things in your life. Positive thoughts can lead to positive actions changing your whole narrative from "I'm a victim" to "I'm an overcomer." Changing your perspective on things can hugely enhance your self-love journey, but also when you seek support from people who can truly catapult you into your greatness.

This all started with me seeking therapy on the day of my marriage separation and receiving a recommendation for a mindset coach who could identify with my current struggles at the time. The craziest thing is that the coaching recommendation was from another ambitious mom I had met years ago at a professional conference. It was the best gift I could have given myself! My therapist and mindset coach helped me learn and recognize how I needed to become more vulnerable, heal old wounds and to help others by sharing my story.

I remember my first day of therapy, I showed up dressed to impress, makeup and hair flawless. I did not look like what I was currently going through. Truthfully, my therapist admitted that I wasn't presenting how she thought I would. The reason why I booked therapy during the start of separation was that I knew at some point my beautiful mask and armor was going to crack. My facade was going to be known and everyone would know things that I had kept hidden while suffering in silence. One of the biggest lessons I learned through life coaching was helping people through my podcast by being my authentic self despite the naysayers. It doesn't mean that you're going out there specifically to be a therapist to others but sometimes it could simply be living your life and being an example of what's possible. This is immensely inspiring and powerful. Better yet, helping women look at themselves with grace and recognize that there are wounds that still need to be tended to. Opening their minds to seeing that they can still move forward and start putting sutures in those wounds and keep on healing. This one is worth repeating here:

"You are the average of the five people you spend the most time with"
- Jim Rohn

So, it is essential to evaluate your circle and stick with people who will help you become better. There comes a point in life whereby creating healthy boundaries and releasing negativity are non-negotiables to your well-being. Self-development can be hard but once you do take those baby steps and start moving forward it can lead to big leaps. You'll see! It's the power of letting go of being perfect and having unrealistic expectations of yourself. It's also seeking wise counsel from those who have already been in your shoes that can then help you navigate the waters faster because their tests have now become testimonies that will help you to go further. This is the way to becoming unstuck because when you practice humility and embrace support from others it helps you get up out of the mud quicker. Remember that lotus? Therapy helps you unpack your old past trauma generational wounds and all those things that have caused pain and discomfort in your life. Life coaching helps you go out there and grab your future version of self and guides and encourages you to move forward, knowing that you're not carrying the baggage or weight of your past.

A Space of Gratitude and Healing

It is a conscious decision to live in a space of gratitude, especially when life doesn't seem to be going as planned. I have personally seen how finding something to be grateful for daily can change your whole outlook on your situation and life! It has been said that your rearview mirror is small for a reason, so you can glance back and look at it occasionally. But your front view mirror is big because your future has so many more opportunities. Don't you just love that? So, if you are continuously looking in your rear mirror and looking at your past, you will not be able to focus on your future. This is where a life coach comes in. They are the wise counsel that helps you to be able to see your blind spots and helps you refocus forward. The therapist helps you to allow the big things that you were staring at to become smaller, all the while you become healed intentionally.

> *"Remember things happen for you, not to you." - Me!*

This is a big mantra that I adopted which helped me stay in a space of gratitude.

Journaling your journey and taking little moments of prayer will also help you embrace gratitude as an integral part of your healing journey. After life coaching and therapy, I also found value in reading self-development books and began journaling my journey. I also purchased a gratitude journal, and I was intentionally writing down three things every day that I was grateful for to keep me in a space of gratitude, humility, and gratefulness. I realized healing and becoming whole were vital to becoming your best version of yourself.

> *"Life is a journey, not a destination" - Ralph Waldo Emerson*

Give yourself grace as you continue to define your life and its new normal! Remember life has peaks and valleys, so embrace each season you are in because there is always something you can learn.

CHAPTER 8

Forgive Yourself

Positive Self-Talk

I began to make it my mission to be with positive intentions, thoughts, and actions in every area of my life. This also included being my own authentic self and letting go of the victim mentality. I made post-notes of my top affirmations and scriptures. Then I placed them in plain view all over my house and phone to keep me encouraged because as you know, the way you talk to yourself is especially important when you are in self-forgiveness. It is giving yourself that gentle internal validation and silencing your inner critic. This can look like doing daily affirmations or devotionals. Anything that will keep you in a space of loving yourself and not neglecting yourself.

When you're trying to go through the metamorphosis or growth process, it requires motion. So, when you're doing growth in motion it means you have to keep moving. You have to keep evolving, and looking forward and when all those things are happening, you have to keep on telling yourself positive things. Speak to yourself as you would to a best friend, or your child.

Keep growing, keep going despite what anyone else says. Quieten the other voices and let your voice be the loudest in your head. When stuck in a victim mentality, your inner critic speaks loudly that you are stuck. The conflicting thought is that you want to become unstuck. When you become unstuck, it's like an acknowledgment that you're in a place and space that you don't want to be in anymore. Think of how palm trees sway back and forth but they never break because they have grown in such a way to weather the storm. You can see the same concept when you look at the caterpillar stage of the metamorphosis process. Caterpillars are fragile and require growth before going into the cocoon. So, as a bruised caterpillar, you recognize that you are yearning for something more in your life. Caterpillars begin to eat, that's how they get fat and plumped up. At this point, you're the caterpillar feeding your mind, body, and soul with positivity. This could be reading self-development books, journaling, praying, fasting, and listening to podcasts. All of these tools you're consuming are expanding your mindset, which changes your perspective and manifests better things to come into your life. Caterpillars are preparing for their next step in the process, the cocoon. When caterpillars get to a point where they stop on the tree, they end up going into the cocoon phase. When are at the same stage, you too have gathered up all of the tools and information that you need to know before entering the cocoon. Now, you must put things into action and do your work. The work being: what is your purpose in life? What are your vision and goals? And this is when You realize that you are now going through the phase where it is time for the transformation into the butterfly.

Move Forward with Acceptance

"But Lot's wife looked back, and she became a pillar of salt."
- Genesis 19:26 NIV

I had made an executive decision that I wanted to move onward with my life. I no longer wanted to keep rehashing my past and living in a space of resentment. No more stuck looking in the rearview mirror! Resentment leads to bitterness. I wanted to become the best version of myself and not be like Lot's wife in the Bible; salty and paralyzed with fear. I had learned how to shake those offenses off like Jay-Z's iconic line, *"Get that dirt off your shoulder."*

For me, this meant having forgiveness for myself and accepting my new normal. Certainly, my life didn't look how I envisioned it would look, but I had become so optimistic in the knowledge that God had something better for me. I can now say that I am living in my truth of optimism. There is power in manifestation and being obedient to God's purpose on your life.

I also had to forgive others. It was probably the hardest thing that I had to do because I was so hurt and angry from multiple hits of betrayal and foolishness from comments and the behavior of family, friends, associates, and co-workers. Can I just say though, as hard as it was, forgiving them freed me, and allowed me to move forward with acceptance. It felt like a big burden released off my back. My spirit felt lighter, and I bloomed into something people had never seen before because I had been doing the work during my isolation period. It was lonely at that time. It was tough, but I learned the most about who I was and had the opportunity during this time to recognize God is my source for everything.

> *"We delight in the beauty of the butterfly, but rarely admit the changes it has gone through to achieve that beauty." - Maya Angelou*

When caterpillars transform, especially when they go into the cocoon, are remolded and changed into something totally different. Ironically, they need all the food and knowledge necessary, so they can figure out the next steps and embrace the isolation period. For us, this starts with changing our perspective. Changing your perspective from no longer the victim to the overcomer. I no longer wanted to be stuck in anger and bitterness toward others and living in basic survival mode. I am no longer staring in the rear-view mirror but looking forward to my future. Soon you will be able to look at yourself from the lens of self-reflection and identify what thoughts are needed for you to be happy and stay in the present, looking forward while building a dream life.

Let Go of What No Longer Serves You

During isolation, I began to evaluate my environment and in particular, the people I surrounded myself around. As discussed earlier, it is essential that you spend time with those who build you up, not bring you down. I realized at one point (and sometimes this can take some time to figure out but usually our gut knows when it is time to move on), that I had outgrown some people and as hard as it was, I had to let them go. They weren't necessarily bad people; they just didn't belong in my next chapter of life. I released the guilt and shame I had from being in the storm at that time. I am grateful for the life lessons because just like I explained with the rosebush, pruning is imperative for maximum growth. I wanted to flourish in life, so I temporarily had to go through my own wilderness period of isolation. I was stripped of my titles, people's opinions, shame, and toxic thought patterns. Holding onto things that are meant to go can be more damaging than forcing something that isn't working. I was loyal to others, but not to myself, which is called people-pleasing tendencies. That's a powerful statement because a lot of people don't realize that loyalty has an expiration date at times and so do relationships. You can't be loyal to someone if they are hurting you or stopping you from moving forward in your life.

> *"People come into your life for a reason, a season, or a lifetime."*
> *- Brian A. Chalker*

Try to look at the time you shared as meant to be for that time. Think about what you can learn from the relationship. You will have more relationships as you continue to move forward. This all goes back to looking at things from a different perspective and being intentional about how you operate and navigate your life. When I was loyal to others and not to myself, I think I got to a point of resentment because I had high expectations for those relationships. I felt like I deserved the same back that I was giving to them. And that's fair enough! But in my life, the lesson that I learned though that is people have their own agendas, thoughts, and actions. The bottom line is people all have their free will. Limit your expectations of people and focus on showing up as your best self. Accept others for who they are and what they are showing you at that time.

> *"When someone shows you who they are, believe them the first time."*
> *- Maya Angelou*

As I continued to develop myself, I came more to the place of examining remorse versus resentment. Remorse is a place of living in acceptance and acknowledgment of your participation in that area of your life. Resentfulness leads to bitterness but also leaves you stuck and in the victim mentality. Did you see how I showed you the difference between resentment versus remorse? Remorse allows you to keep going and allows you to live in forgiveness because forgiveness is for you, not for them. Being better and leveling up to your best self is so much better than being bitter and holding onto anger and disappointment. That's why sowing positive seeds into your mind will facilitate actions that will affect how you show up in your life. More than anything this will become a reflection of how you treat yourself, how you treat others, and how they treat you, in return.

CHAPTER 9

Self-Belonging (Joy and Wholeness)

"Build Gates, Not Walls"

You might be keeping out people who can water you, so you have to learn how to have gates and not walls.

When you build gates, you allow good things to flow in for you and allow what doesn't serve you to flow back out. When you are healing, there is a tendency to become hardened and block out everything, like a wall, because of fear of rejection or hurt. And that's understandable. But how does that help you? I have now grown to open my heart space by knowing that I could be blocking things that are actually healthy for me. It is better to think of boundaries as a gate. Some things can come in; healthy things. Some must be kept out. Boundaries are key here because you teach people how to treat you. Having unhealthy boundaries can lead to you letting unhealthy aspects/people come through that gate and the result can leave you becoming resentful for allowing things and accepting things that you don't want. But it's up to you to keep that closed, or, recognize when your boundary has been crossed and make sure you put boundaries in place so that it doesn't happen again. I can't stress the importance of boundaries enough to you. They are ways to protect you and they show people what you will and will not accept. They also protect your precious heart and energy. I can honestly say that my boundaries were blurred in my work environment and with close family members which caused much unhappiness in my life, mostly as a result of trying too hard to belong. At work, I wanted to be considered a great employee and continue to flourish in my career. With my family, I wanted to be dependable, loyal, and trustworthy. Everywhere else it was easy for me to enforce my boundaries. You actually belong anywhere you go because it is a thought!

> *"You are only free when you realize you belong no place—you belong every place—no place at all."- Maya Angelou*

As discussed earlier, establishing healthy boundaries also means learning how to let go of people, things, and places that no longer serve you because they are not in alignment with the boundaries that you have set up for yourself. Even if this is hard. In essence, others can be holding you back from reaching your full potential. You are holding onto what feels comfortable with the fear of not belonging anymore. This can also be an issue if you are a people-pleaser. People-pleasers tend to conform to the environment to keep things neutral and safe and they want to avoid conflict. At all costs! The silence of not speaking up for yourself usually is a sign that you have a lack of inadequate boundaries. I encourage you to get clear on your own boundaries and stand firm on them because they will become your compass as you continue to navigate and have joy in your life. Watch people who become uncomfortable when you begin to enforce them. Some people will be happy, but there will also be people who are upset when you begin to choose yourself more and prioritize your well-being. Some people can't get a handle on it. Others need a little time, and that is okay too. Give them time. No one likes change or finds it easy. Especially if they have many insecurities of their own. I have personally witnessed this in my personal life and professional life.

However, I am so proud of myself and glad I made the decision to choose myself more by building gates!

Adversity Can Lead to Opportunities

> *"The thing is that we are wired to be a part of something bigger than us so deeply, that sometimes we will take fitting as a substitute, but actually fitting in is the greatest barrier to belonging because fitting in says, 'Be like them to be accepted.' Belonging says, 'This is who I am'"*
> *- Brene Brown*

Girls growing up, especially women of faith are taught to be seen and not heard. And also, not to cause friction and just do what you are asked to do. Everyone wants to have a sense of belonging to something. Over time, these limited beliefs, however, can spill over into other areas of your life while in your pursuit of professional success. I tolerated more microaggressions than I care to talk about because I wanted to belong or prove my worth.

In society, it is truly hard to be a mother and have a career; it can be frowned upon. I knew when I was younger that I wanted to have a career and family, but it did lead me down a path of burnout. The reality is that I was living in survival mode and code-switching to fit in.

The highly demanding job left me feeling so drained and stressed from tolerating toxic behaviors of people at times, not to mention taking on the rollercoaster of emotions from patients and their families. The high pressure of knowing that one mistake or error could kill a patient is something that I think about every time I move to a patient's side. It may have caused some PTSD and probably is the leading cause of my hypervigilance. On the news, we hear so much about medication errors, bad patient outcomes, and people losing their professional licensures. I am very intentional and focused and great at the services I provide to my patients, but sometimes it can lead to burnout if self-care is not incorporated. Burnout can also lead to mistakes, which is also something to keep in mind.

When I was a critical care nurse, I had one supervisor who would always give me the hardest patient care assignments and give my co-workers easier assignments. I used to get so upset because I didn't like being treated unfairly and being overworked. When I questioned this treatment, the supervisor denied the mistreatment and stated that I received these assignments because they thought I could handle it. My question was - at what cost...my health, well-being, time, etc.? However, another staff member noticed and reported these unfair actions. I have faced many obstacles due to my age, gender, and race in professional settings. In hindsight, it made me a stronger critical care nurse because it built my endurance and knowledge base that would serve me for the rest of my professional career. Fast forward to over a decade later, and I consider myself to be a confident and competent advanced practice registered nurse while trailblazing the future for people to come behind me! It is not easy to break the mold or be the first person to get in the door! The thing is, I was lucky to be able to move through all this. Some are not so lucky, and burnout has killed their career and damaged their personal lives. I don't want this to be you.

PART THREE

MINDSET GROWTH

CHAPTER 10

The Power of Cocoon Work

The power of immersing your mind with positive thoughts to weed out the negative thoughts is key to a growth mindset. Cocoon work is representative of the metamorphosis process of the caterpillar going into the cocoon. When the caterpillar goes into the cocoon, it is preparing for isolation and transformation. Remember this is a process, it is inevitable in order to become a gorgeous happy and fulfilled butterfly.

We can learn many things from watching nature and animals go through life.

Baby Steps Lead to Big Leaps

> *"You have to be uncomfortable in order to be successful, in some ways. If you stay in your comfort zone! You would never do the things that you need to do." - Lights Poxlietner*

Let's look at our mindset. A mindset shift occurs when you proceed to take baby steps that will lead to big leaps. Think of it as standing by a stream with stepping stones laid at your feet to help you make it across to your destination. It becomes the necessary process or path to success! But first, you must take that first step. It will be uncomfortable initially but keep going. I was uncomfortable about showing up on camera and doing live events because I'm a very low-key and private person. I remember when I started my social media, including my podcast cover; it did not include my face. Now, you can find me all over the internet using my voice, but also showing my face. This allowed me to be my authentic self but step out with the courage to move past my comfort zones with boldness and confidence. I want this for you too! It feels so great!

> *I believe your tribe will recognize you when you show up for yourself and don't shrink to make others feel comfortable. It becomes a whole vibe, for sure!*

Transforming your mindset will become easier over time if you consistently show up and make a conscious effort to be intentional. Allow yourself to lead with more vulnerability and self-awareness. This will help you regain your sense of identity and learn who you truly are. Your mindset and heart space are everything when it comes to building your dream life and coming out of survival mode! Realize that your thoughts lead to feelings that will ultimately lead to your actions. Be careful about those pesky ruminating thoughts because they have power over your life and the path to success.

Comparison to Others and Identity

Don't compare yourself nor be consumed by your titles and roles in life because you may confuse this with being the source of your identity. Your 'who' is different than your 'do!' This means who you are is not defined by what you do in life (roles, positions, etc.). I had to learn this lesson the hard way when I hit rock bottom in life by recognizing that I was defining my own self-worth and identity into what I could provide for others. As I share this with you, I can recognize that I was operating out of the intentions related to acts of service to show my support and love. I would then become very upset when my positive intentions were not recognized or appreciated. When I let these false narratives go, that is when I bloomed into knowing that my value was always complete, and my identity was not defined by the many roles I play in life. All I had to do was show up as my true authentic self and that I am enough just like that!

> *"I praise you because I am fearfully and wonderfully made; your works are wonderful, I know that full well." - Psalms 139:14 NIV*

We can become so very engulfed in what other people are doing and sometimes miss our own blessings. Racehorses ride with blinders on their eyes to help them stay focused on running their own race. In other words, try to let go of the comparison spirit and focus on your own race in life. Because that just gets you all mixed up and creates more negative thoughts about yourself when you compare yourself and start thinking you're good enough. Stay away from too much social media if it makes you feel this way! And remember, your self-worth is everything; you are good enough. And once you know who you are in Christ, you really are going to be doing the darn thing. Embrace where you are right now and do self-reflection. This will allow you to begin the mindset-shifting process. It will be uncomfortable!

> *"We're limited by the thoughts we choose, our character can be summarized by our thoughts. If we think the same, we will be the same, and we will have the same thoughts" - James Allen*

Transformation takes time. And you can't judge how long each part of the process takes. You may fly along at one point, then slow, or even be at a standstill at other times. Keep going. I mean, my process could take a few years and yours could take a few months; that doesn't make my process any different than yours, it is whatever time you need to be where you need to be. That's what you do. Start prepping for your plans. When you get it in your spirit, you have to say that you believe in yourself; you have to be patient with yourself. You have to start setting some goals. That's why I said once you know what you want, then you can set goals to achieve them. Change the behavior that's not working for you. Get your wings stronger, be thankful, and discover your limiting beliefs. You'll become unstuck and gain clarity at the crossroad to release yourself from the cocoon. Life coaching is for your future. Be aware of your past but decide fully to focus on what lies ahead! A coach will help propel you forward. It's preparation and application. It's growth and transformation into something totally different, and of which no one can see the internal work in progress.

CHAPTER 11

Purpose and Vision

What is Your Purpose? What are Your Passions?

If you're expecting something to change, you have to change your attitude, your demeanor, and your thoughts; everything needs to change. As a result, you're not going to be continuously having the same results because you're not doing the same thing. As we dive more into this, let's talk about purpose. Purpose, when you do a literature review on it, is a goal or an intention, hence why my podcast is called 'Intentional Queen.' Then you go into your vision; a vision being the ability to plan for the future. This gives your purpose a direction. Thoughts are everything when we dig into our purpose. So, we're going to dig more today.

How do we intentionally set, and renew our mind, on our purpose and our vision and be that "Intentional Queen Thinketh;" pulling some inspiration from James Allen's book. You just have to change your thoughts! Everything is either a positive seed or a negative seed, and we want to change the bad ones. We don't want weeds thriving, do we?

> *"Every thought-seed sown or allowed to fall into the mind, and to take root there, produces its own, blossoming sooner or later into act. Good thoughts bear good fruit, bad thoughts bad fruit." -James Allen*

I know my purpose is related to my gift of teaching and speaking. I mastered how to continue to have positive self-talk dialogue because I knew at some point, I would be beginning to speak life into others. However, it wasn't until I recognized my self-worth and dug into my passions that I would soon stumble upon the purpose God had set out for me to do. It takes time but even more so, courage and self-belief that you are on the right path in your pursuit of success and true happiness within. It is truly a journey, but my humble beginnings, nursing career, podcasting, and coaching have definitely been the fruit of me blooming into the woman I am today. I want you to bloom too! And I know you can!

Birth Your Vision

Let's dig more into your vision. Birthing your vision is where action takes place once you start living out your purpose. I highly encourage you to have a vision board, or simply just write down what you want; get all those things down on paper. There is something that makes it clear and obtainable when you put your pen to paper about your intentions. They become real, you become accountable.

> *"And then GOD answered: 'Write this. Write what you see. Write it out in big block letters so that it can be read on the run. This vision-message is a witness pointing to what's coming. It aches for the coming—it can hardly wait! And it doesn't lie. If it seems slow in coming, wait. It's on its way. It will come right on time..." - Habakkuk 2:2-3 MSG*

Once you create your vision board, now we need to try to create a lifestyle that changes things for the long term. So, remember how I said your mind is like a trained muscle. Well, you have to get it in your head that you're going to meditate on the things that you want. Let's relate it to the process of pregnancy. It takes nine months, unless you have a premature child; nine months to carry a baby. It's a process, the baby's not fully grown until it hits maturity closer to the ninth month or third trimester. You too, are in a process; it takes time, and it needs time. But look what you get at the end!

Let's talk about some nurses out there that are reading this that can relate. There's the Benner's theory where talks about a novice nurse moving to being the expert nurse. When I came out of nursing school at the age of seventeen, I would be considered a novice nurse with minimal experience. And, over twenty years out, I am ranked as an expert nurse because of my years of experience and training over time. The point is, over time you become wiser by activating your skillsets and recognizing what stage you are in.

> ### *"You can't explain a giraffe decision to a turtle." - T.D. Jakes*

Here's a funny story for you. I did an interview with my friend on another podcast, and she saw me sipping my giraffe cup. And I have giraffes everywhere around the house because well, as you know, what you think about can also include affirmations and the things you put in front of yourself. So, giraffes are big to me. The reason what he was saying there is about viewpoints or sight lines. A turtle and a giraffe, one animal is not better than the other. But the vantage point is oh, so different. A giraffe has a very tall neck, it has vision, and it can see far. But a turtle is a little lower on the ground, right? And it can only see from its viewpoint.

> ### *You are a giraffe in these streets. You have vision and will go far in life!*

Now, a giraffe's big heart pumps all the blood to flow up to his neck; it rarely comes down, meaning its neck rarely comes down but only to get a drink of water every so often. When it leans its neck down, that is a risky time for the giraffe because it is when the risk or the vulnerability is the highest of getting attacked. But when they've bent down briefly, because they need nutrients and they need water, they need to level up again. And so, when you put this all in the scenario of a typical person's life; you have people who see a vision. These people want the vision for other people, so they lean their necks down to help them to help themselves. And sometimes, they get into that vulnerable state for too long. And then if the blood flow can't go back up their neck, they pass out. And if they pass out, then they become at risk for damage or danger. So, sometimes you can't explain to somebody a vision that God gave to you, because they can't see it from the level that you see it. And you can't stay down there too long trying to get them to see it at the risk of your own life.

I can say from my personal life, that I saw a vision for others. I told them, look, you're going to be so great if you do X, Y, and Z. And they're like, "Jineen, I don't see it." Well, sometimes I was trying to bring them up with me on my vision or my flight. And they weren't down for it. They couldn't see what I saw. But I was endangering myself by sticking my neck out in certain places that I shouldn't have done, because it put me too far at risk of getting harmed. And if you want me to be a little more candid on this, which you can see, I don't hold back in my honesty on your journey, sometimes you can get bitten by a snake and not even know it was in your camp. So, you have to be careful when you are sticking your neck out. In the streets, as I say, that's my little lingo, 'in the streets', you have to be careful when you're out here because you can turn around and get endangered and don't even know it because you're not watching your whole 360-degree view; you only see the first part of what is ahead.

Now that we've talked about turtles and giraffes, let me be clear and make a disclaimer, I have no issues with turtles! Because I am a nurse, there is a nursing sorority that I belong to. And the turtle is our mascot. And it represents perseverance and that slow and steady wins the race. Turtles are awesome, in that sense. So, let's not take that out of context. But for what we're talking about today, a giraffe represents vision, foresight, and dreams and moving forward into those dreams. Now you know why I have giraffes all around me! Giraffes are like my spirit animals; kind of funny when

I'm out doing my side business. My patients know me by my hat; I had a special scrub hat made in giraffe print. You know, everybody is rocking the leopard. I had this special giraffe hat made and when I'm out, that's how my patients remember me. And they're like, "Hey, you are the one who wears that giraffe hat!" And I'm like, "Yeah, because it's my spirit animal!"

I use the inspiration of the giraffe for insight or vision, because pretty much when you're thinking things and you're changing negative those thoughts and mindsets, you have to train it like a muscle. So, you have to continuously see it's implanted in your mind of what you're thinking and what you're doing. And I wanted to say to myself, I have vision, I have vision, I have vision. And so, I put it everywhere to remind myself; girl, you got vision.

CHAPTER 12
Embrace Your Journey

What I've learned going through this journey is that restoration and happiness is not a destination, it truly is a journey. So, people ask me how I came up with the title of this podcast. It took a lot of thought. But when I really started boiling down to where I was trying to go with this, I knew that restoration is in it, and that's why it is called 'journey to restoration.' And it's intentional because we are being deliberate about how we're going to do it, and how we're going to get to where we need to be so we can level up each other.

Sometimes you have to meditate, get yourself out of that negative spirit and get something positive in you. Sometimes you have to reset your mind and feed it with better thoughts. I have truly embraced every step of my journey because I know that it is for a purpose and on purpose! I watch motivational videos and speeches often. They have been a pillar in my mindset growth and birthing my vision.

One day I was watching Tyler Perry on a motivational video. He was discussing how to keep praying and maintaining while on your journey in life. And so, what he said is that when you're up against challenges and storms, the way to get through them is you have to pray. So, you can go higher and then you maintain that level until you get to the next one and you pray and maintain, and you just keep going higher until you get closer to your vision or your vantage point, like a giraffe.

Schedule Your Worries

Sparking joy and having gratitude are essential to embrace your journey, especially when things are not going as you expected. It is easy to get into a rut and a depressive state. But don't stay there; figure out what makes you happy. When I did the women's empowerment night event, I started off with an icebreaker question; what's something that brings you joy, excites you or gives you energy? And the women gave me so much insight about that. We also talked about their current stressors and struggles that were holding them back from joy and productivity in life. Once we dug into these stressors, the women gained clarity about some things that were bothering them by becoming more vulnerable. I was able to coach these women in how to lead more into self-care and self-love. But it was our thoughts about our stressors that led to how deep we were able to go and how vulnerable we are and being able to encourage and level each other up. In essence, it was about promoting community and stopping each other from suffering in silence.

And sometimes the worry that we endure; is just a moment in time.

Schedule some worrying time, especially if you've got a lot of stuff on your plate with your stressors. You know, sometimes you must just schedule that time rather than having it constantly swim around in your head. Give yourself a time, then give yourself a break till then. So, you'll say you know what, I'm going to deal with this crap later tonight, between nine and ten when I put my child to bed; whatever it is. You're going to have to sometimes schedule your worries because you can't walk around holding the weight of the world on your shoulders every day or being so consumed in your problems that you can't enjoy the little things because sometimes, it's just a moment in time. Don't let it be your whole day, your whole year!

*"I have not failed. I've just found 10,000 ways that won't work." -
Thomas Edison.*

I'm going to call to action for you guys now to reset your mind.
Embrace where you are in whatever stage you're at in your journey. Avoid
distractions, know your limits, and create those beautiful boundaries!
And no matter what, every step is important in your season because it
creates experience. Don't be scared to fail. Think about Thomas Edison;
how many times did he have to fail in order to succeed? It was thousands
of times before he became successful at what he brought into the world.
Remember, you are winning or learning. So, you just get back up and let's
shift your crown together.

CHAPTER 13
Live in Your Own Truth

Living in your own truth stems from living in authenticity and manifesting a life you dream of with joy and intentionality. Living in your own truth is borne out of the thoughts you have; positive or negative. And living your own truth can also be decided by level one being caught up in daily distractions and by sinking into procrastination.

We all want to have a dream life without resentment and guilt! We all just want to be happy and enjoy everyday life! But in order to achieve that goal we must sow positive seeds into our minds and watch them bloom into reality.

> *"Happiness can only be found if you can free yourself of all other distractions." - Saul Bellow*

Some time ago, I was watching a movie starring Morgan Freeman. He was giving great advice to one of the characters in the movie. It piqued my interest because Morgan Freeman handed the guy the book, 'As a Man Thinketh' by James Allen, and told him to read it. The other character was a guy who had been wrongfully accused of rape. Next, Morgan Freeman says, 'Why don't you draw this picture?' This is the same powerful concept of using affirmations, or drawing a picture and placing it on my mirror for around two months straight.

This process is always going to be a circle; with two lines down the middle. In the middle, the two lines represent distractions. And the reason why it's a circle is because you're trying to become complete, your full self. And if you keep allowing yourself to be shortcut down the middle by the distractions, you'll never make your way fully around the course to be your full self. So, once I put that little diagram up, that's how I was able to deal with distractions and say, you know what, this is trying to distract me from what I'm trying to do, and it would bring me forward around the circle. It sounds simple, but it really works! We must keep focused on what we need to do and not allow the noise to distract us or where we're going. And it's okay to become distracted. It's our ability to bring ourselves back into focus that matters.

> *"To expect the unexpected shows a thoroughly modern intellect." - Oscar Wilde*

As you know by now, I used to have such high expectations of myself and others. And I mean, I used to be offended by things that I shouldn't even be offended by simply because I was expecting others to do things and behave in such a way as if they were me. And if they didn't, I thought that after hearing my advice, they would! But what I realized was; that they're not me. I'm not them, and I can't expect them to be like me. And so why am I sitting over here getting offended because they're not responding or behaving the way that I would expect them to if they were me? That was heavy. That was a big wake-up call.

I then chose to 'expect the unexpected' where I started eliminating expectations of things and people and letting go of perfectionism. It gave me more inner peace and an overall sense of calm. What a weight off my shoulders trying to help everyone! Of course, I can still help others, but they will only act when they are ready. We can lead the horse to water…! Over time it allowed me to be courageous and start doing things without expectations. In essence, not shrinking myself and focusing on positive thoughts.

> *I began to focus on progress over perfection!*

PART FOUR

BLOOMING INTO YOUR SOFT WOMAN SEASON

(BUTTERFLY TRANSFORMATION)

CHAPTER 14

The Power of a Positive and Intentional Mindset

Blooming into your 'Soft Woman Season' takes intentionality and changing your perspective of how you think in order to manifest the life you want. Transformation happens when you are deliberate and take actionable steps in every area of your life. Truly getting yourself out of survival mode and 'never losing yourself again' takes being consistent, but also remembering your journey and loving yourself along the way. This is why I love butterflies so much, because of the transformation process! It is the journey – we can take the pressure off ourselves knowing that it will take time, just like a gorgeous butterfly.

What thoughts are you having on a routine basis?

As we know, thoughts will influence how you operate from beat to beat. Consider looking at your thoughts like negative or positive seeds. Positive seeds help promote growth and transformation, whereas negative seeds can cause decay or deterioration of growth. Negative thoughts can limit you and keep you stuck in spaces that you want to get out of. They can also inflict guilt and shame. Don't worry, we have all been there! I remember having negative thoughts and feelings when I was going through some painful moments in my own life, such as, "I am not good enough", "Why is this happening to me?", "What are people thinking about me?", "Am I a good mom?" We really can torture ourselves!

The power of the mind is so fragile!

With thoughts like those, I began to slip down the slope of hopelessness and resentment. No wonder! However, I remember enrolling into therapy and beginning to deal with my past traumas and issues. It wasn't easy, but I made the decision to want to be in a better space; I no longer wanted to be stuck in survival mode. I also invested in a mindset coach for high-achieving black women! She has been a tremendous help, and also a certified registered nurse anesthetist like me, so I felt comfortable as she was able to identify my common struggles during that time. She encouraged me to change my perspective, but more than anything she gave me that push I needed to become a mindset coach and self-love expert for ambitious moms who struggle with overwhelm and self-neglect and who, like me, want to experience more peace, wholeness, and confidence in their daily lives! In other words, I wanted to help high-achieving women and moms bloom into their own soft woman season and incorporate more self-love!

During this journey five years ago, I decided to process my past and do quite a bit of unpacking. I made the choice to lean into positive self-talk and support myself with affirmations. It was a gift to myself and my life! With practice, I was able to cast down any negative thoughts on the spot and replace them with something that better served me at the time. This will forever be a journey, but the goal is to recognize when your brain wants to lean back into what is more comfortable. Simply acknowledge the thought and be compassionate. However, reaffirm yourself in a positive manner.

Intentional thinking is sometimes best performed when you are operating with vulnerability and stepping outside of your comfort zone.

Have grace in that space! I can truly say now that all the things that I have endured and witnessed were intentional because they have served me! They served me well in preparation for the life I deliberately wanted to create for myself and my family. Building a legacy and being in the public eye can be quite terrifying, but when you know God has taken you through the boot camp, you can have some relief. I believe he won't give you more than what you can handle. It took me a couple of years to publicly put my face on social media! But it got easier. Also, I push myself to do events and speak out about my truth! The rewards for overcoming my fear are huge. Now my sheep, my dear flock, know my voice because I own my true authentic self.

> **But look at me now as a testimony to you of the power of a positive intentional mindset!**

This year is a big year for me! I'm ending a decade of my life to start on a new one. I was asked at a recent women's conference about where I see myself in the next few years. I began thinking that in order to start a new chapter in my life, I must begin anew and release the old things that no longer serve me. The purpose of your rearview mirror is for you to glance back, remember where you have been, and stay in a space of gratitude. Keep going and moving forward into your Soft Woman Season! The goal is for you to not stay stuck in your past because that is something you cannot change. Focus on what is within your control and let the other things go! Once you embrace authenticity by being true to yourself you will then become clearer about Who You Are!

As a mindset coach and podcaster, I overcame my own issues with authenticity when I realized how to let go of my titles and embrace my identity as a Child of God! I began to step out on faith and changed my perspective about myself; showing up for myself and realizing that I was cultivating the Intentional Queen Tribe! Women and men were tuning into the podcast to hear me speak every other Thursday. It was wonderful!

Women wanted to coach with me for a reason and get the results that I had proven within my own journey! I was proof that it could be done. I had the tools to share. It was all falling into place beautifully. I was helping others to never lose themselves again by becoming more confident and whole while building a dream life on their terms!

> *There's a difference between being confident and courageous versus having a high level of self-esteem.*

Your self-worth, (who you are), is not the same as how confident you are! When we get wrapped in our titles and objects, we think that it determines our worth because our lives are flourishing (mom, wife, co-worker, etc.). The goal is to not consume yourself and put your identity into the things that you do versus knowing who you are. When you really get clear about your values, standards, and boundaries, you learn who you are! And you learn that is enough. Also, you may not look like who you had been when you show back up in places and spaces with people who knew you in the past. Be the role model to help someone else through!

> *Realizing your people need to find you, but how will they find you if you don't show up!*

I started the Intentional Queen Podcast approximately three years ago, and after launching the podcast for the first three months. As mentioned earlier, I didn't tell anybody that I knew personally. I needed God to show me that this is my purpose and how to be obedient in something that I had never done before. So, I showed up consistently every two weeks and people kept coming, which positioned me for more blessings. This helped me expand into life coaching and networking with like-minded people. I am honored to have helped thousands of women via my podcast and mindset coaching by showing up for my tribe!

You may not look like what you have been through! Remember, a butterfly does not look like a caterpillar, nor like it was developed in the cocoon. However, each stage requires work and the ability to transform into something new along the way! But first, it starts with your thoughts in your mind. I consider myself to be your accountability person and give you my cheat codes to help you get through your stages quicker with me by your side! I am my own living testimony. So, if are you struggling to balance busy mom life with your career and everything else in life, you are in the right place, and in safe hands; let me help you too!

CHAPTER 15

Purge and Release: What No Longer Serves You

Purging and releasing that which no longer serves you gives you the capacity to take on more things that you want to do. It's awesome! Think of it as decluttering your closet and home for spring cleaning. Take the pieces that are left after you purge and begin to build the life you want on a solid foundation. Your ego is something that can get in the way of embracing your Soft Woman Season. It can be sneaky but also like to take a front-row seat in your life when you feel offended. I used to be the person who when I was offended or triggered, would let my ego drive the car without brakes. I was the 'comeback queen' that was going to tell you off for the offense. However, when you do this, you allow the other person to control you. They then take your power away.

> *Make sure to protect your peace at all costs, mentally and physically!*

So, this means getting better at picking and choosing your battles wisely. Allow people to think and feel whatever they want about you! It's of no consequence to you. Choose to respond versus being reactive. Take a beat and learn how to respond when your emotions have settled. Lead with a cool head because words are something you can never take back. This is a skill to practice while becoming more confident in your current situation. Letting go of the ego and coming out of conflicts with your power still intact will allow your life to shine bright. You will begin to run your own race! Remember that comparing yourself to others can be so detrimental to your psyche. This is why racehorses run with blinders on their eyes, so they don't become distracted from their own goals and paths in life. Let's adapt that into our own lives! Your ego is your sense of protection, but when you become more confident in your truth and live on your own terms, you will not be easily distracted by the insecurities of others.

I have learned that silence is golden!

People simply cannot argue or fight with you if you do not engage in their foolery. I have dealt with my own toxic relationships in my personal and professional life. This has served me well when dealing with these types of people in my life. When you refuse to engage, they will soon get the message that you have established your boundaries and love and respect yourself on a deeper level. This is a true reflection of knowing your self-worth and the value you bring to the table in every area of your life. It's letting go of people-pleasing and betraying yourself to make others feel happy and comfortable. It's embracing your Soft Woman Season; releasing you from these things that no longer serve you. So, purge them today! Be in a space of gratitude about how these things have helped you in the past as building blocks into your future.

Keeping it moving!

Confidence will begin to bloom when you continuously show up with courage and vulnerability. Vulnerability helps you connect on a deeper level with yourself and others.

However, you must first become transparent and get to the root of who you truly are. This leads to being unapologetically yourself and living in authenticity! The deep-rooted aspects of ourselves that we hide from others can also be the things that block us from reaching our full potential.

As mentioned earlier, when I was seeing my therapist, I was well-dressed, and from the outside, I certainly did not look like I was going through an ugly divorce and grieving a family member. My therapist was shocked that I was going through this because I seemed so well put together on the outside. Truth moment: I booked my therapist because I knew I was going to need support when I truly became vulnerable and was ready to unpack the recent events. Sometimes, you have to think ahead and consider what you need and become proactive. My therapist still shares her first encounter with me till this day. I believe you should have a therapist and coach at every stage of your life! Therapy is such a great tool while you are on your journey to restoration.

> **I was a very private person and lacked vulnerability in most areas of my life.**

At work, I was living a different life and as a high-achieving woman, it's common to live two separate lives. You have to be a boss and author-itarian at work in order to be respected by your employer. On the other hand, you are expected to be warm, caring, and submissive at home. It can be challenging trying to operate in both arenas with a sense of balance, with endless patience and energy. The biggest lesson I learned was that so many ambitious women fear vulnerability in their corporate arena for fear of not being taken seriously in their roles. This was mind-blowing to me because I too felt the same way.

After my mindset shift, I now operate as my true, authentic self in all areas of my life. Nevertheless, the key was establishing and maintaining my boundaries. Boundaries are so important in every area of your life. Remember they are for YOU; not to control others. You will become more comfortable enforcing your chosen boundaries by practicing them on a daily basis. Make sure to watch the people who are upset when you enforce these boundaries because they were the ones who were benefiting from you lacking them. This will help to make your pruning and purging process easier because you will now be clear about who, what, and where to let go.

Initially, it will be overwhelming, but take things one step at a time!

How do you eat an elephant? Not in one gulp but one bite at a time! Overcoming overwhelm has so many layers to it. But I think sometimes when we are overwhelmed, we turn into procrastination. Or, we have perfection-paralysis kick in because of the need to be perfect! Also, we may lack vulnerability, but that's all until you begin to unpack! It's until you get down to the root! It's until you recognize what needs to go, what needs to stay, or what needs to be altered. Some things need to be repaired, not necessarily thrown away. Then there's things that need to stay, but it's spending the time with yourself for self-reflection that aids in this process. This could be journaling, getting a coach, speaking to a therapist routinely, or all three.

The inner work needs to happen. You want it to happen! You acknowledge all of this by becoming self-aware! Then the next step is going in and doing the inner work, which is cocoon work. This is when you may not look like what you've been through because a butterfly does not look like what it went through when it was in a cocoon. Affirmations are key during this time and it's definitely crucial for your self-belief. As you know, I say my affirmations daily and put them on a notecard in my bedroom. Think of affirmations that resonate with you, write them out and post them up. You may like to include the affirmation: *I do not look like what I've been through, but it does not discredit what I've been through. It shows healing and growth in a journey of hope!*

Letting go of functioning in perfectionism was a game-changer.

Letting go of perfectionism released me from the added pressure and shame I would feel when I wasn't performing to the caliber, I envisioned for myself. I realized that completion to the best of my ability is good enough! Perfection-paralysis refers to when you are expecting everything to be perfect because you don't want anyone to say anything negative about your work performance. In essence, you are trying to control their thoughts, feelings, and actions! You cannot control other people's thoughts, feelings, and actions because that is on their side of the table. All you can do is control yourself! Perfectionism is also a people-pleasing tendency because you conform to others around you! You want people to think of you in a certain way or people to respond to you a certain way; but the reality is you can't control their thoughts! Accepting that fact and losing some of those perfectionistic tendencies will help you stop neglecting yourself and bring more peace to your life. I believe when you become whole and heal, this will become easier to let go of.

> *Investing in yourself daily is imperative to your mindset growth and manifesting the things you want in life, but first, you must take action.*

Nevertheless, perfectionism can precipitate the pressure of trying to alter ourselves and not recognizing grace for ourselves! It's about saying you are enough today but there are things that you can work on! God made us perfect in his image and likeness, but there are of course things that you could improve on! And when you accept that you're good today and you're going to be good in the future, you have some space to think about what you can do gradually to get closer to the person you want to become. There is so much power in letting go! Reclaim your own power while embracing your Soft Woman Season.

CHAPTER 16

Create a Work-Life Balance and Develop a Support Team

Overcome Overwhelm and Self-Neglect

Creating work-life balance is important as you embrace your Soft Woman Season. When your life is chaotic and unbalanced, it will lead to burnout. We've already touched on overwhelm, but let's dig a little deeper. Many high-achieving women and mothers are experiencing overwhelm, which leads to self-neglect. Shame and guilt usually are some underlying feelings that leave you stuck on the hamster wheel of life, continually running from here to there, juggling a million things and getting mentally fatigued. And it's because I have experienced health issues from a lack of balance in my life, that I want to help you to avoid getting to such a low point. More importantly, self-care and establishing healthy boundaries are imperative to overcoming overwhelm. Also, aim to focus on one task at a time! I was the 'queen of multi-tasking' and wanting to be superwoman to everyone in my life except me! Yes, except me! I even experienced a work injury that had me questioning my career choice. During that time off with my work injury, I gained a new perspective about how and why I was showing up in my life this way. I wanted healthier relationships in my life, but I realized that they must be nurtured!

Rest is considered an act of self-care and self-love!

Your family and friends will thank you for taking some time out to rest and recharge because you'll be less irritable and easier to be around! It reminds me of the Snickers commercial where it says, "You're not yourself when you're hungry". You are also not yourself when you don't get rest. When embracing your Soft Woman Season, know your capacity and limitations of what you can handle during that time. Make your needs known to the people around you, and please let them help you!

In the past, I was one who wanted to do everything myself and not depend on others. This stemmed from my past pattern of choosing certain people who didn't have the capacity to help me, which left me having trust issues with most people helping me. During my wholeness journey, I realized that I was giving too much of my energy into people and things that didn't have the capacity to do the same in return for me. I had to learn how to forgive them and myself. Changing my perspective about understanding that they have their own things going on or they just didn't have the capacity to help me in the same way and at that moment. However, I could have chosen to ask people who *could* help me versus who I *wanted* to help me. I now recognize that to have a work-life balance, it meant that when I'm not at work I need to check into being present in the moment at that time whether that's with my family or friends. I guess in essence, it's that cliche of leaving work at work and home at home.

Overcome overwhelm by focusing on one task at a time!

I have learned that multitasking, even though I say I'm good at it, is not the way to a peaceful state of mind! I have found it is less stressful to focus on one thing at a time, so I can better direct and harness more of my energy instead of being distracted with multiple activities. My productivity sky-rocketed because I was able to complete more tasks and feel like I accomplished more, and to a higher level, too!

Another tip to combat overwhelm is where I encourage my clients to take actionable steps and I hold them accountable to their desired goals. So, identify your top three daily tasks and schedule them in your Google Planner or paper calendar. Commit to completing one task at a time, allowing yourself to fully engage with each activity. Block out time for self-care and breaks to ensure you're maintaining your well-being. Experiment with working during your peak brain hours (e.g., mornings) when distractions are minimal. Keep your phone out of reach during work hours and select a focus-friendly environment. I implore you to think about areas in your life where you can try to create some more balance even if you have to carve it out on your calendar and make time.

Building a tribe and having a village is something that will also help you when you're trying to create some work-life balance as an overwhelmed and ambitious mom. When you allow people to help you it takes stress off you to tend to other things and really just learn how to not be in that total superwoman syndrome that comes so easily to us. It's a top priority in your self-love and growth mindset journey! The people you surround yourself with have the ability to influence your life and decisions in a positive or negative manner. Make sure you choose carefully out here in the streets! I remember my parents used to tell me to be careful with the company I kept around me and now I have greater respect for that statement as an adult. Keep in mind that people will judge you also by the people you keep on your team because it says a lot about you as a person.

I have learned to stand on my values and honor my boundaries.

Two of my top values are intentionality and integrity. I stand on them as a blueprint and in every area of my life. These two values have helped me through multiple struggles and crises in my life. Keeping them at the forefront of my mind has helped me make decisions that were aligned with my vision and purpose. Having a word of the year can also be very helpful and powerful and can be looked at as having a compass of knowing where you're going, especially from year to year. However, if you don't know what you're standing on, such as your standards and values, you will be lost and conflicted.

Quality Over Quantity

Throughout my journey, I have gained more clarity in knowing the people that I surround myself with have also helped me with discerning whether they are helping me to grow or if they are hindering me from getting to my next season. I want you to look around and analyze the five people you spend the most time within your life. If they are not prospering or moving forward in life, this is the time you have to question your surrounding environment and decide if they are going to be on your team.

I've had to feel this combination of purpose but also pain when I had to decide to let some people go in my own life. But ultimately, when I decided to be more vulnerable, it helped me to attract the type of people that were for me and that were also helping me become the better version of myself that I am today. You want to be around people who are like-minded and share similar goals and aspirations. Nevertheless, you don't want to be the smartest in the room because you will hit your ceiling of growth. So, choose wisely with the five people you spend the most time with; you want to be leveling up and glowing up in these streets! This means that there's a higher chance of you becoming like the people you interact with the most, especially if they are positive influences! During your Soft Woman Season, you may start off by taking better care of yourself and decreasing your overwhelm. Less stress leads to more inner peace, especially when building a support team to help you accomplish your goals! Getting on social media, support groups, creating accountability partners, and networking at women's events, were all game changers for me in establishing my outside community of other ambitious women to support me as I am leveling up to my next season.

> *"As iron sharpens iron, so one person sharpens another."*
> *- Proverbs 27:17 NIV*

I started the 'Intentional Queen Journey' because I wanted to build a community that empowers all women to become the best version of themselves on their self-love, self-healing, and growth mindset journey! Three years later and counting, I am writing a book about my journey to help inspire you to keep going and take care of yourself along the way.

Being a mother is one of the best things that has ever happened to me. And through some of my darkest moments, it truly was God and my son who watered me. Your children can sometimes give you purpose, gratitude, and drive to want to improve yourself personally. I am grateful for the roots on my tree because you only need a few of them. They're the ones that are unseen, but they keep you alive during your pruning and your roughest seasons. I tell my clients during coaching that I want to be a branch on their tree as an extension of support to them, and to let them know that I am a part of their tribe!

> *Nobody likes to feel alone, support is necessary for growth!*

I like to "Speak to the one". This means consistently showing up for yourself and for the one person that needs you! It's so important to show up because your test will become testimonies that are blueprints for people who have been through what you went through. Sit with that a moment! Your lessons and truths will become the knowledge you teach others who are in the seat that you once sat in. Most importantly, the place that you have overcome and bloomed out of; just like a butterfly coming out of its cocoon! God can use this to show you that what happened to you was actually for your own good; giving you the ability to relay back the lessons you have encountered, and give people hope to keep moving forward! Let them know that they are not alone!

> *In the cocoon, you are alone but it's a temporary season for growth.*

Have an intentional mindset that starts within you and positive thoughts that you ruminate on a constant basis. Once you know who you are and what you do, then you'll be able to attract and manifest who you want in your life to compliment you and go on to the next level with you. In books, there are chapters for a reason. Some end and some start, but they are all a part of one book. I encourage you to look at life in that same way. You must have chapters and seasons that will end and start, but they all contribute to helping you rise from broken to beautiful.

CHAPTER 17

Give Yourself Grace and Know You Are Enough

Talk to Yourself Nicely

We've talked a bit about the power of having positive thoughts. Let's go into this a little more. Self-talk shapes your mindset, well-being, and self-belief for achieving your goals and building your dream life as an ambitious mom! If you ever catch yourself falling into the trap of negative self-talk, suffering in silence, and dealing with guilt and resentment, this one's definitely for you! These are proven strategies from my signature framework! Here is how I can help you dive deep into the transformative process of releasing self-sabotaging habits and creating a more positive and empowering inner dialogue. Because Sis, the way you talk to yourself sets the tone for everything else in your life! Become aware of your inner dialogue and identify self-limiting beliefs. Challenge negative thoughts and replace them with positive affirmations.

> *"Talk to yourself like you would to someone you love."* - Brené Brown

Positive "sexy" self-talk is a must! I remember in the past saying to myself, *"Jineen, we're going to do better, now we have to do better. I want to do better"*. Talk to yourself nicely. When you cultivate positive self-talk, it changes the whole narrative of how you talk to other people, too. And what I really realized from some of the people that I've encountered over my life, and even recently, is that how they were speaking to me wasn't personal. It really was how they were talking to themselves on the inside. Why? Because they probably had those thoughts multiple times before those words popped out their mouths. That's how it works! So, giving them grace in that space is imperative. Recognize that praying for them is a better choice rather than becoming bitter by mistreatment. Everyone has internal battles that they are facing.

> **When you are focusing on the things you can control, you begin to have a life of joy and happiness.**

This also stems from having self-acceptance and self-control. When you can control your thoughts, actions, and how you speak to yourself, you will become unstoppable! You begin to step into your purpose and take your power back. Get clear on your intentions of talking to yourself nicely and of wanting to do something versus having to do something. When you tell yourself you "have to" do something, it can create pressure, drama and a negative connotation which in turn can lead to procrastination, self-doubt and resentment. Tell yourself, "I want to…" because it creates endorphins and gives your body a sense of encouragement to step out of your comfort zone and take actionable steps towards your goals in life. It also makes you take responsibility for your decisions rather than putting the blame on others, which tends to leave us miserable and feeling helpless or resentful.

I believe in the thought of 'just hurry up and fail already' because it will give you the data and space you need to attempt to pivot while trying again. It's something you can birth but if you never try, you will never know. The goal is to never give up trying but also recognize when you have hit a wall of insanity. It's knowing it is time to stop versus quitting.

Tell yourself you have tried your best and keep going. Make sure to love on yourself more. Know that you are worthy of love, and you are enough! Remember that it starts within you! Your mind, your thoughts, your actions, and so on. How are you viewing yourself? Make sure your lens is accurate!

> **It is so key to speak Life into yourself EVERY DAY!**

More on affirmations: practice daily affirmations and visualize yourself succeeding in your goals. Here are some of my favorite affirmations. Feel free to adopt a few or all into your daily life.

- Be better and not Bitter.
- Don't be like Lot's wife out in the streets (dust off offenses).
- Move onward and forward into my vision and purpose.
- Stay in my lane and drive my own car of thoughts and actions.
- I am a Queen and I do things with good intentions.
- I seek God first in everything (Matt 6:33).
- I have a vision and I am manifesting it into reality.
- I am loved, smart, worthy, and a child of God.
- I sow good seeds in order to reap my Harvest.
- I will trust the process and ordered steps.

Embrace Healing and Wholeness

Wow, I love the word resilience! I am truly a believer in lotus flowers because they have to come up through the murky water and still shine beautifully! I always talk to my clients about the power of release and letting go of what no longer serves them! Sometimes, you have to lose to gain! Look at how rose bushes must be pruned back to flourish in their next season. I would say I have had life experiences that resembled these analogies. My pruning was beneficial because it made me stronger and more beautiful in this season. I believe life is like seasons, too; winter and fall are when things look rough and scarce. However, in spring and summer, you are in bloom!

> *"Life has all sorts of hills and valleys, and sometimes you don't end up doing what you had your heart set out on, but sometimes that's even better!" - Ruth Buzz*

There is a common story in the Bible about Ruth, Boaz, and Naomi. The story goes that Naomi was helping Ruth get in position for her destiny. Sometimes you don't know what God's doing, but he may be positioning you in certain spaces. He may make things happen that way, so you can rest for preparation. That's a heavy thought that I used to struggle with, especially because I had a lot of perfectionistic tendencies; of building success even if it's at the detriment of my health. I was going to succeed by all means necessary, and at the detriment of losing people (and myself), too. But it eventually got to a point that it wore me down mentally and physically. I was in the valley of my rock bottom. Now, you can see how to rise and bloom where you are planted. I became more self-aware and reflected on how I had reached that low season in life. Everyone has those seasons, so you are not alone! But don't give up; embrace your journey because soon you will have more fulfillment in life.

> *This is how I started to regain who I was because I had lost myself.*

- Cultivate emotional awareness and mindfulness to understand your feelings.
- Learn healthy coping strategies to manage stress and challenging emotions.
- Seek support from a network of friends, family, or a supportive community.

- Surround yourself with supportive and positive individuals. Minimize exposure to negativity or toxic environments.
- Engage with uplifting content, books, podcasts, or videos.
- Embrace new experiences and challenges to stretch your comfort zone.
- Face your fears and see them as opportunities for growth.
- Gradually increase the complexity of tasks you tackle to build confidence.

The goal is to BLOOM where you are planted!

Confidence Unleashed

I'm going to be really transparent and vulnerable right now. I heard an inspiring message from a past sermon. It was about how God can send you away in order for you to come back better and more confident. When I was recently injured, the decision was made that I could only return to my active duties if I was confident and competent. This had me a little discouraged because my injury prevented me from being able to work at my peak performance! I had endured many treatments and medical care to help me get back on track. I remember I had reservations after being away for half of a year because of my chosen career path. It was during that time that I learned to rest and remember the other moments He showed me what to do. All my needs were met; not to mention I had more time to spend with my family. This is how God is so good! I had many people who spoke negatively and full of discouragement over my return. Little did they know, my comeback was personal, and I had God with me.

But, when you know God will be your vindicator and has the final say in the situation, you will become a victor!

This pertained to many areas in my life. Your story too, will become a testimony to help others.

I wrote this book during my six-month period of rest. When you listen to the podcast, it's me coming back for others. Your tribe will recognize you and show up because you have to help them. God can send you away and you don't understand at the time. But he wasn't saying not to return, he was saying, 'not right now.' You have to come back after the cocoon work, just like the butterfly. Take your time, then observe how the isolation period has a profound purpose in your life. You may be experiencing self-doubt and may be torn about where you are going with your life. I know you want to become more confident, and you want to elevate while on your journey. Remember it's a journey, it's not a destination, so there are still things you will continue to work on along the way.

> *"Believe you can and you're halfway there." - Theodore Roosevelt*

Self-doubt can be a mood killer. This can result in feelings of mom-guilt, resentment, low self-worth, and a lack of fulfillment. Ambitious moms may put the needs of their families and others ahead of their own, leading to a neglect of their own self-care and personal growth. Believing in yourself builds courage and confidence. Remember, your belief in yourself is a driving force that propels you towards achieving your goals and building your dream life! Define your aspirations and set ambitious yet achievable goals. Break down large goals into smaller, manageable steps; taking action towards your dreams will boost your confidence. Seek internal validation. Become more grounded in who you are and not your roles in life. Don't let your titles become your idols.

Maximize Your Life's Toolbox

Think of your life like a toolbox with lots of different tools inside. Each tool has a special job. The important thing is to figure out which tools you have and how they can help you fix the problems in your life. For example, in motherhood, I'm teaching my son important tools such as being open, and authentic, showing respect, and having confidence. These skills will serve him well as he blooms into adulthood. I want him to be responsible and learn how to do things on his own. This is a special nudge to my own parents for giving me the blueprint as I continue my own parenthood journey. Knowing which tool to use is like knowing when to use different medicines for patients in my nursing career. Sometimes, you need a very specific tool, like a special kind of medicine, while other times, you just need something simple, like Tylenol for a headache. Life is like a journey with ups and downs, and knowing which tools to use at the right time is the key to success. It's like choosing between a flathead and a Phillips screwdriver when you need to fix something. I like to use stories to help you understand because I want to inspire your spirit and soul to succeed.

CHAPTER 18

Time is Valuable: Live an Impactful Peaceful Life

Activate Mindfulness in Motherhood

To be mindful and powerful, you need to come out of your shell like a butterfly and make your dreams come true. Don't be quiet to please others, because in the end, being in control of yourself is like having a superpower. It's like a muscle you can make stronger by dealing with your strengths, things that bother you, and your limits. When you stay calm and focused on your goals, you become even more powerful and outside distractions won't stop you from reaching your dreams.

Grab yourself a piece of peace!

At one point, I listed all my gifts and talents, but most importantly, I realized that time is valuable! Your kids grow just so fast; it feels like a blink of an eye. I learned how to be present in the moment with my son. We had more planned quality time that was devoted to us bonding without outside interactions and interruptions. I remember I surprised him at an in-school activity that parents could attend. He was so thrilled and excited that I was there. One thing about being a healthcare worker is that it has a demanding work schedule. I had missed out on many things for him when he was younger due to my work hours as a nurse. If you are a high-achieving woman and mom, you know the struggle is real!

Superwoman syndrome is so common in motherhood!

We are trying to be everything to everybody. When we take on all these tasks without taking care of ourselves or resting; it's a straight line to burnout. As a single mother, I am guilty of this too! The goal is to release the superwoman syndrome and take off that cape! Better yet, throw it in the bin! Start saying "No" to the things that no longer serve you or can be postponed to another time. Carve out time for regular self-care activities that rejuvenate your mind and body. Engage in physical exercise that you enjoy, such as yoga, dancing, or walking. Nourish your body with proper nutrition, hydration, and sufficient rest.

It's a time for growth and abundance.

Sometimes, making your dreams come true can be a bit messy. You might wonder what's different in your thirties compared to your forties and how it relates to being a woman. I've learned some important lessons on my journey. One big lesson is getting comfortable with feeling a bit uncomfortable, and thus being more open with my feelings. I used to be a very private person and tried to please everyone, even if it meant putting myself last. I talk about my experiences on my Intentional Queen Podcast.

Being a people-pleaser can make you forget about yourself and make yourself smaller to make others happy. This can lead to a lack of true connection and vulnerability. I coach women to understand the power of being open and setting healthy boundaries. These boundaries are for you, not for others, and they help you become brave and confident. Now, you can shine bright and stop shrinking in different parts of your life. We all have special gifts and talents, so it's important to be there for yourself and your community and share those gifts.

I'm entering a new decade soon, and I'm manifesting a wonderful 2024 as an Intentional Queen!

CONCLUSION

Balancing a career, being a mom, taking care of yourself, and growing as a person is like a delicate dance. It might seem tricky, but it's very much worth it. When you change the way you think and love yourself on purpose; it's like magic. Your work life becomes better, too. You can ask for more money and things you need for yourself and your family. When you're your best self, absolutely everyone benefits, and you become the best you can be. Even if shining bright feels scary, it's important when people need you.

There's a story in the Bible about a woman named Esther. The crown chose her to do something important. She didn't choose it, but she was there for a reason. God put her in the palace to save her people. She needed courage to stand up and do what she was meant to do. Don't make yourself small to make others comfortable. You have something special that others need to see.

Many women feel confused about their life paths. I've been there too, but therapy and life coaching helped me figure things out. They gave me the chance to be my best self and build a strong future. Always remember, you are enough just as you are today. Don't let anyone tell you otherwise!

Self-love means speaking kindly to yourself and sharing that kindness with others. Sometimes, it's important not to stay in places where you aren't wanted or that don't make you feel good. Rejection can happen, but it can also be a good thing if you look at it in the right way. As you now know well; loving yourself deeply, healing, and becoming whole is like a caterpillar turning into a butterfly. It might take time, but it's worth it. All the hard work you do gives you tools in a toolbox that help you on your journey. You'll know when to use them with the help of God, and they will make you feel free. Keep going on your intentional journey and have faith that your future will be better.

Helping others starts with healing yourself and setting goals. Remember to take breaks and take care of yourself. You don't have to be in survival mode all the time! Believe in the power of making your dreams come true. Don't let what others think stop you from being yourself. And don't work so hard that you forget to enjoy life.

Embrace the journey and be intentional in everything you do. Focus on healing, loving yourself, and being the person God meant you to be. Let go of perfection; just make progress. You're a great person, and you are loved. Step out of your comfort zone little by little, just like taking small steps.

It's important to set clear boundaries and make sure people are respectful in your life, whether they are your friends, family, or co-workers. When you do this, they will like the happier and healthier you. Being yourself and sharing your true feelings with others can help you shine and make the world a better place. You can inspire people and be a positive influence.

Remember to take care of yourself, learn, grow, heal, be mindful, and become more confident on your journey. It's important to focus on both self-improvement and self-care. Level up your Intentional Queen to a better you!

And lastly, don't forget to stay connected through social media, podcasts, and emails, and be a part of our community. We'd love to meet you!

ACKNOWLEDGEMENTS

First, thanks to God, without His strength and love, I would not have a story to share. My adversity has taught me that my gift will make room for me. He is my strong tower and a place of refuge. This book is my story that will inspire and impact change for the women who are coming behind me on their journeys to restoration. I am grateful for this next chapter of life.

To my son, I love you forever! This book will be a keepsake of my story to share with generations to come. Please know that being your mother is one of the best things God has given me. Remember to love yourself first, so you can love others genuinely.

To my parents and siblings, you are the roots of my tree. You have witnessed the ebbs and flows of my life. You have seen me conquer it all, but most importantly, you never left my side. You have been my biggest cheerleaders along the way. Mom and Dad, you told me I would write a book about my life. I did it! I love you all, especially for the support you give my son!

To Latorsha, our friendship and sisterhood has evolved over two decades! Your support in helping me find my voice through podcasting has changed my life. Using my voice has helped me transform other women's lives as well. Thank you for being the person I needed when I was in some of my darkest moments. You have also instilled the importance of self-care.

To the Intentional Queen Tribe, I thank God for you. This includes everyone that I didn't get to mention because the list would be too long. You have supported me from the moment I birthed my vision of the Intentional Queen Journey. You have shared your own transformations with me, which lets me know that God makes everything happen for a reason. No longer will you lose yourself or suffer in silence.

ABOUT THE AUTHOR

Jineen, a mindset coach and self-love expert, helps ambitious moms alleviate overwhelm and self-neglect by guiding them to experience more inner peace, confidence, and wholeness. Along the way, she empowers them to incorporate more self-love into their journey. She is also the host of the Intentional Queen Podcast: Journey to Restoration with Jineen! Her podcast has helped her become a motivational speaker at women's events and retreats.

Five years ago, she hit a pivotal moment that required her to make some significant decisions within a short time span...divorce, health issues, and the loss of family. She had hit her own rock bottom! She was neglecting herself, struggling with self-worth, lacking inner peace, and having Superwoman syndrome. After recognizing things had to change, Jineen went on a personal mission to restore her life to wholeness. Plus, she vowed to never lose herself again by learning how to choose herself more often.

Jineen's life now includes being a certified life coach with over 20 years in the nursing profession. She enjoys being a boy mom and promoting women's empowerment. Jineen has been featured in *Canvas Rebel* and *Shoutout HTX* magazines for her expertise in women's empowerment and personal development. She has cracked the code with her proven framework to stop neglecting yourself, know your self-worth, live a life of more ease and peace, and love yourself on a higher level. Jineen truly believes in high-achieving moms who want to have it all, recognizing that balance and self-belief are key! It starts with you! Currently, Jineen has helped thousands of women build their dream lives through her mindset coaching and podcast. They have gone from survival mode to the soft mom life, vowing never to lose themselves again!

Facebook, Instagram, TikTok, and YouTube: @Intentionalqueenjourney

Website: Intentionalqueenjourney.com

NOTES